The Existence of "Things" and the Eternity of "Site"

KISHIO SUGA

菅 木志雄 〈もの〉の存在と〈場〉の永遠

HeHe

ごあいさつ

岩手県立美術館では、2009（平成21）年度から岩手県ゆかりの美術家を個展形式で紹介する企画展を開催しています。このたびは「開館20周年記念 菅木志雄展〈もの〉の存在と〈場〉の永遠」を開催いたします。

　岩手県に生まれた菅木志雄（1944-）は多摩美術大学在学中から作品を発表し、60年代末から70年代の日本に起きた美術動向「もの派」の作家として活躍しました。もの派の活動が終息した後も、様々な手法による作品を発表し続け、今日まで日本の現代美術をリードしています。さらに近年では、海外の著名美術館での展覧会や作品収集が続き、世界的にも注目を浴びています。

　菅の作品は、並べる、曲げるといったシンプルな行為を加えながら、石や木、金属等の日常的な素材を空間に置いたり組み合わせたりすることによって、素材同士や置かれた場所、さらには人との関係性を考えさせるものです。既成概念を取り払い、独自の哲学のもと、「もの」と「場」の本質を掘り下げることで、従来の美術の在り方を根本から問い直しました。この制作姿勢はもの派の頃より今日まで変わることなく続いています。

　また、静岡県を拠点に制作を続ける菅ですが、70年代以降定期的に岩手県の画廊で新作を発表したり、岩手県立美術館で大規模な作品を制作したりと、故郷で生み出した作品も少なくありません。これらには、次への展開を予期させる作例も含まれ、菅の制作歴の中でも興味深い一面を示すものです。

　本展では、岩手で発表された作品を含む、インスタレーション、レリーフ、ドローイング、写真、記録映像など多岐に及ぶ約120点の作品を、10年毎の時代に区分し通覧しながら、菅の半世紀以上にわたる制作活動を振り返ります。

　最後になりましたが、本展の開催にあたり、多大なご尽力をいただきました菅木志雄氏をはじめ、貴重な作品をご出品賜りました各所蔵家の皆様、ご後援、ご協力を賜りました関係各位に対し、心より御礼申し上げます。

主催者

Foreword

Since 2009, the Iwate Museum of Art has held a series of solo exhibitions featuring artists who have ties to Iwate Prefecture. On the occasion of the museum's 20th anniversary, we are pleased to present "Kishio Suga: The Existence of 'Things' and the Eternity of 'Site.'"

Born in Iwate Prefecture in 1944, Kishio Suga began exhibiting his works while a student at Tama Art University and was active as an artist in the Mono-ha art movement that emerged in Japan from the late 1960s to the 1970s. Even after the Mono-ha movement came to an end, he continued to produce works using a variety of techniques and has been a leading figure in Japanese contemporary art to this day. In recent years, Suga's works have been exhibited and collected by many renowned museums across the world, earning recognition on a global scale.

By placing and combining everyday materials such as stone, wood, and metal in a space while intervening with simple actions, such as aligning and bending, Suga's works prompt us to consider the relationships among materials, the sites they occupy, and people. Doing away with preconceived notions and delving into the essence of "things" and "sites" based on his own singular philosophy, Suga has fundamentally reexamined the nature of conventional art. His approach to creating art has remained unchanged from the time of Mono-ha until the present.

While Suga continues to work from his base in Shizuoka Prefecture, he has also created many works in the region where he grew up. Since the 1970s, he has regularly shown new pieces at a gallery in Iwate Prefecture, and created large-scale works at the Iwate Museum of Art. These works include examples that anticipate subsequent developments in his practice, and thus represent a fascinating aspect of the history of his creative output.

This exhibition looks back at more than half a century of Suga's artistic practice through a selection of some 120 works, including pieces shown in Iwate, covering a wide range of media such as installation, relief, drawing, photography, and documentary film, divided into ten-year periods.

Finally, we would like to express our heartfelt gratitude to Kishio Suga for his extensive efforts in organizing this exhibition, all the collectors who agreed to exhibit their valuable works, and all those who kindly offered us their assistance and cooperation.

The Organizers

目 次 | Contents

在るのでもなく、無いのでもなく

美大をでてから、いくつかの個展をしたが、このときすでに従来のイメージ操作
による制作を否定し、もののリアル性と場の構築性に視野を移していた。田
村画廊やときわ画廊での個展は、自らの思考を具現化したものであった。これ
らの作品の延長線上に東京や京都の美術館での展覧会がある。わたしはこの
頃〈もの〉とそれらがある〈場〉のはなれがたき一体性をどのように提示すべき
か、寝ても醒めても考えていた。〈もの〉があれば、必ずそこに〈場〉がある。
どちらが欠けても作品は成立し得ないとわたしは考えていた。〈もの〉のリアリ
ティは〈場〉のリアリティでもあった。パリ青年ビエンナーレやヴェネツィア・ビ
エンナーレにおいても建築の空間性や構造性を無視できなかった。それは岩手
の盛岡合庁別館での仕事も同様であった。わたしは〈ものハ〉といわれ、自ら
も〈ものハ〉というが、これは表現スタイルをいっているのではなく、生きるた
めに世界とどう向き合っていくべきか指し示すものなのである。だから一過性の
ものではないのである。

菅木志雄

2021.8

Not Being Present, Not Being Absent

After graduating from art school, I held several solo exhibitions.
At that time, I already rejected the convention of creating
art through the manipulation of imagery, and had shifted my
perspective towards the reality of things and constructedness of
sites. My solo exhibitions at Tamura Gallery and Tokiwa Gallery
were manifestations of these thoughts. Those works evolved
into subsequent exhibitions in Tokyo and Kyoto. In those days, I
kept thinking, even when I was asleep, about how to present the
indivisible oneness of "things" and the "sites" where they exist.
Where there is a thing, there is inevitably a site. I believed that
a work could not take shape if either of them were missing. The
reality of "things" was the reality of "sites." I could not help being
aware of the spatiality and structuredness of the architecture at
the Biennale de Paris and the Venice Biennale. The same was true
at the annex of the Morioka District Joint Government Building
in Iwate. I have been called a "Mono-ha" artist and I have also
referred to myself as "Mono-ha," but this does not denote a style
of artistic expression, rather it indicates how to engage with the
world in order to live. It is, therefore, not transient.

Kishio Suga
August 2021

〈もの〉と〈場〉 —— 菅木志雄の世界

建畠哲

昨年の菅木志雄の個展カタログに掲げられた『放たれた景空』と題されたステートメントは、作家がこれまで長年にわたってさまざまな視点で論じてきた〈もの〉と〈場〉にまつわる問題をもっとも簡潔なことばで集約した注目すべきテキストである。

〈もの〉があるというとき、そこに必然的に〈場〉があるということを考えなければならない。〈もの性〉と〈場性〉は、背中合せのものであって、どのような状況においても離して考えられない。〈もの〉を認識しているとき、〈場〉も共に意識の中に入れているといっていいだろう。（・・・・）ものはいわば一点集中的に、〈場〉に存在しているが、場は、もともと非実体的な様態によっていると思われるので、もののように視るというわけにいかない。しかしながら、〈もの〉の存在が消えさらないかぎり、〈場〉は、歴然として、そこにあるべくしてある広がりとしてあるのである。また逆に〈場〉があるからものはあるべくしてある姿を保ちつづけていられるといってよい[1]。

ここでいう〈もの〉と非実体的な様態によっている〈場〉との関係は、まったくの素人談議を許していただければ、物理学でいう場の理論、粒子同士が直接的に相互作用するのではなく、場を通して作用しあうという理論を思わせなくはない。（上記のテキストの英訳では〈場〉は "site" とされているが、場の理論の〈場〉は英語では "field"、フランス語では "champ" であり、菅のいう〈場〉も「ある広がりとしてある」からには、"site" に加えて "field" や "champ" に近い意味合いをも含んでいることばといってよい。）

〈もの〉があるとき、そこに必然的に視ることのできない〈場〉、非実体的な様態によっている〈場〉が背中合わせのものとしてあるという考え方は、実のところ菅のインスタレーションの作品に一貫しているのであって、初期のテキストである『状態を超えて在る』（1970年）も、考えようによってはすでに別のことばで同じような認識を示していたといえなくはない。物が状態を超えて在るとは、「物が一般的にある状態から極限としての『在る状態』を認識する」[2]ことである。なにやら禅問答のようだが、それは〈もの〉が不可視の〈場〉と背中合わせになっているからからこそ、〈もの〉がただある

のではなく「あるべくしてある（極限的に在る）」姿を認識しうるのだと解釈できなくはない。

1999年に書かれた『領域は閉じない』は "領域性" や "周囲" ということばで自らのインスタレーションのありようをより詳細に論じたテキストである。

インスタレーションは、モノそのものと同時に、そのモノのある領域性（領界性）を見せるものである。領域性は、空間の性状に準じているが、どちらかといえば、その領域内に存在しているものによって、その性格づけをあきらかにすると思われる。たとえばブロンズの人像があれば、それを受け入れる空間（人為性を含めて）として、逆に自然風土の中にあるもの、石とか樹木であれば、それらが生きづくような空間となって、領域性を特長づけているといってよい[3]。

インスタレーションがモノ同士の空間的な配置構成による表現でもなければ環境的な表現でもなく、「モノそのものと同時に、そのモノのある領域性を見せるもの」とされるなら、場性と領域性は同一視できないにしても深く重なり合った概念ではあるに違いない。

*

具体的に作品を見てみよう。本展に出品される初期の作品《斜位相》（1969年）（cat. no. 2, p. 23）は2本の角材を互いに斜めにもたせかけて立たせただけのシンプルな作品で、床に接した部分は、どちらも小ぶりの2個の自然石が柱を挟み込むように置かれている。

ものが極限的にある状態とは、それが日常的な事物であれ作品であれ、いかなる意味も付与されていない無名性の状態をいうものでもあるだろう。

《斜位相》における木材の組み合わせは単純な物理的な重力の働きに依拠したものであり、石の配置も含めて、もたせかける、床に置く（初出は屋外であったようだが）という状態をリテラルに示しているだけで、造形的な意図とは無縁なインスタレーションなのである。

ではこの角材と石という〈もの〉が明らかにする領域性と

はどのようなものであるのか。

　あるテキスト（1997年）で菅は「わたしはあえて、〈見えないカタチ〉というものをひとつの認識の対象として、とらえる必要性を感じている」と記している。「ある構造を組み立てるとき、視野をさえぎることのない開いた空間を考えてもおかしくはなく、それでもって、全体のモノの在り様を察すれば、〈見えるところ〉と〈見えないところ〉が入り混じり、全一なるカタチ（領域）ができあがるとしてもあやまりではないだろう」[4]。

　これは先の菅の場の理論の祖型をなす考え方といってよい。「それを見るニンゲンの視点が、〈見えるところ〉いわば閉じた構造にむかうのか、あるいは〈見えないところ〉、いうなれば、開いている空間にむかうかによって、モノの在り様がちがうし、受けとる内容も別のものになる。（・・・・）わたしは、開かれた構造のところは、そのままモノの〈周囲〉につながっており、ときには、どこまでが構造で、どこからが〈周囲〉なのか、正確な判断ができないことを思う。その流れで考えれば、〈場〉〈領域〉におけるものの在り方や連関性は、そのまま〈周囲との連関性〉とも考えられ、それが明確に自覚され、組織化されなければ、結局のところ、自らの思考をモノによって、充分に体現できないのではなないかと思われるのである」[5]。

　もし《斜位相》を見えるカタチとしてのみ捉えたなら、それは表現的な要素を一切排除したミニマリズム的な作例と見なされたはずである。だが菅のことばによるならそれは開かれた構造であるところの〈場〉であり〈領域〉であって、そのまま〈周囲との連関性〉を宿していることになる。「〈見えるところ〉と〈見えないところ〉が入り混じり、全一なるカタチ（領域）ができあがる」ということと「〈もの性〉と〈場性〉は、背中合せのものであって、どのような状況においても離して考えられない」ということとは、四半世紀近くを隔てた発言でありながら、ほぼ同じことを言おうとしているのであり、そのような立場はすでに菅の初期の作品において明らかであった。《斜位相》における木材や石は即物的に存在しているのではなく、〈周囲との連関性〉においてあるべくしてあるのであり、それを逆にいえば、ものがあるかぎり非実体的な場や領域は不可避的に発生しているのである。

　《斜位相》の翌年の《無限状況Ⅰ（窓）》（fig. 1）を見て

fig. 1　《無限状況Ⅰ（窓）》 1970年　京都国立近代美術館での展示風景
撮影：菅木志雄

みよう。写真でしか残されていないこの作品は京都国立近代美術館の窓を開き、窓枠に太い角材を斜めの状態で挿入したものであって、まさに"放置"ということばにふさわしい作品のありようであった。

　菅は『〈放置〉という状況』と題されたテキスト（1971年）でこう記している。「私がいう『放置』とは、すでに概念化されてある芸術の認識のなかで、身動きの取れなくなった方法論や、ものや状況の概念を、今までの芸術の体系の外におこうとする意である」[6]。「時としてものの雄弁さは人間の語り口をしのいで、人の想像性よりももっとイマジナティヴになりやすいのであるから、最初にもの自体の持つイマジネーションを抜きさしならぬ状況でぶち壊さねばならないのであった。あげくのはてに私は、ものとその状況を『放置』しなければならなかったのである」[7]。

　興味深いのは彼のいう"放置"がアーティストの主体的な表現の否定であるばかりではなく、「人の想像力よりももっとイマジナティヴになりやすい」「もの自体の持つイマジネーション」をも排斥するためのものとされている点である。ダダやシュールにはじまるオブジェは現代美術でも姿を変えつつ命脈を保っている。菅にとっての放置とはバラまいたり放り出したりすることではなく、そのような呪物的な想像力のありようを退け、ものが極限的に在る状態を直截に認識するために要請された行為でもあるのだ。

　窓枠に挿入された角材の光景は、即物的なものでもなければ謎めいたものでもなく、ましてサイトスピーシフィックなものではなく、むしろ場として開かれた構造をもつというべきであろう。

このような意味での〈場〉を支配する力学が造形的な原理ともフェティシズムと無縁であるとして、ではただ無作為なアナーキーな広がりであるのかというと、それが私たちを深く魅了し続けている他に類例のない〈領域〉であるからには、当然ながらそのようなものではありえない。

インスタレーションではそれぞれのものが等価の主体性をもって求心力を排除するように散在しており「完結性があるようで、ない」と彼はいう。「そのかわり、インスタレーションにおいては、まだ手つかずで場（周囲）を形成しているさまざまなものに内包されている〈複雑性〉や〈多様性〉をそのままのカタチや状態で、提示できることになる」[8]。

これまでは初期の作品を論じてきたので、ここでは2000年の《大地の育成》（cat. no. 87, pp. 74–75）を取り上げてみよう。3本の鉄パイプを組んだ高さ3メートル余りの三角錐を床の上に5つ配したもので、それぞれのパイプの下にはバケツの台座（1本だけは木の台座だが）がある。バケツは他にも幾つか置かれていて、そのうちのいくつかには白いロープが繋がれている。あるいは誤読になるかもしれないが、このタイトルを自然と等価であるような場の生成と読み替えることを許されたい。作品は自己完結的な空間ではなく、場（周囲）を形成する〈複雑性〉や〈多様性〉を内包しており、未だ生成の力学を宿しているのである。

「それは、一本のヒモの端を引っぱって、ついには長い全体を知るごとくである。コトバや文字や文章のシンタックスになぞらえられるのも、当然の成り行きであるかもしれない。ことばの組み立て、文章の配置はどこかインスタレーションと呼応するものをもっている」[9]とも彼はいう。

私が注目したいのは、ここで彼がシンタックスということばを用いていることだ。菅は周知のように秀でた文章家でもある。「インスタレーションといえど、ひとりのニンゲンの意識の動きが介すると、やはり個的な〈世界観〉がかかわっている」[10]。場の力学は決してアナーキーなものではなく、文字や文章同様のシンタックスが働いている。そしてそのことはインスタレーションばかりではなく、彼の平面作品やレリーフ状の作品にもいえることなのだ。

いささか唐突に思われそうだが、私はここで19世紀の象徴派の詩人、ステファン・マラルメの《骰子一擲》を持ち出してみたい。死後に刊行されたこの21ページにわたる難解極まりない詩は、基本的には線行の記述を維持しながらも、それらを細かく分断して配置し、また大小の活字を用いることで、見開きごとに文字の"星座"を成立させている。

マラルメは〈骰子一擲〉のある見開きで「何も起こらなかったであろう、場をのぞいては」（RIEN AURA EU LIEU QUE LE LIEU）と記している（fig. 2）。この「場」が「まさしく〈頁〉の成立に他ならない」（石田英敬）とするなら、頁が書物の中にあってなお自立した場＝フィールドでありうる可能性をマラルメは示唆していることになる。瞠目すべきなのは、そのセンテンスが3つの行に分割され、他の行の中に離れ離れに紛れ込ませてあることであろう。星座＝場を形成する星々（文字）が、自らのシンタックスによってことばとは場の生成であることを語っているわけである。（もっとも先に述べたように場に相応するフランス語はchampであってlieuではない。頁の概念に関わる問題がその違いに潜んでいそうだが、その問題に言及するのは別の機会に譲るしかない。）

ともあれ〈骰子一擲〉とは、ことばと場とが相互的な状態として維持されている名状しがたい何ものかである。牽強付会を承知でいえば、そのことが「〈もの性〉と〈場性〉は、

fig. 2 ステファン・マラルメの『骰子一擲』の「何も起こらなかったであろう、場をのぞいては」というセンテンスが載っている頁、図版は http://www.gci.org.uk/Documents /MallarmeUnCoup.pdf からの転載。

背中合せのものであって、どのような状況においても離して
考えられない。〈もの〉認識しているとき、〈場〉も共に意
識の中に入れている」という彼の発言と照応しているように
私は思われるのである。そう、菅自身が「ことばの組み立て、
文章の配置はどこかインスタレーションと呼応するものをもっ
ている」[11]と述べているからには、それはあながち的外れの
見方とはいえまい。

　（ちなみに峯村敏明は菅の作品のことばとの関係を「音
声が分節性によって言語となるように、モノもまた分節性に
よって言葉に類したものになる」のであって、「菅がモノの
言葉を語りうると見なされるのは、そのことによる」と述べて
いる。「モノの分節は、モノと同水位の空間を分節せずにお
かない」その時、観者は「モノの透明な言葉が、名状しが
たい不透明な存在の詩に変じていることを知るのである」[12]
という峯村の論点は、上記のような場のありように別の照明
を当てたものといえよう。）

＊

レリーフ作品でいえば、近作である《止域》（2016年）
（cat. no. 105, p. 92）や《連場》（2017年）（cat. no.
106, p. 92）は矩形の平面に大小の矩形の板を、方向を
変化させながら連結させ、全体を白いアクリル絵具で覆った
作品である。一見抽象的構成といえなくはないが、タイトル
に域や場ということばが含まれているように、作者の意図は
構成そのものにはニュートラルであり、自己完結的ではなく、
周囲とほぼ同義である閉ざされていない領域（彼にとって
周囲とは中心と周縁といった二項対比的な概念ではない）
にある。

　菅の作品は美術における近代主義（それは造形表現を否
定したコンセプチュアリズムにも観念の表象化として尾を引
いていた）を切り捨て、まったく新たな美術の可能性を切り
開くものであった。初期作品から今日まで、さまざまなイズム
の交代とは無縁に自らの立場を貫いてきたアーティストに大
いなる敬意を表したい。

（多摩美術大学学長）

註

著者は12以外はすべて菅木志雄である。

1.「放たれた景空」『菅木志雄 放たれた景空』展カタログ、小山登美夫ギャラ
　リー、2020年、p. 5
2.「状態を超えて在る」『美術手帖』第324号、美術出版社、1970年2月、p. 29
3.「領域は閉じない」『菅木志雄著作選集 領域は閉じない』横浜美術館、
　1999年、p. 11
4.「周辺を束ねて界端を開く」、出原均、藁科英也編『菅木志雄』展カタログ、
　広島市現代美術館他を巡回、1997年、p. 21
5. 同上書、p. 21
6.〈放置〉という状況」『美術手帖』第344号、美術出版社、1971年7月、
　p. 145
7. 同上書、p. 147
8.「領域は閉じない」、前掲書、p. 11
9. 同上書、p. 11
10. 同上書、p. 11
11. 同上書、p. 11
12. 峯村敏明「人はソレをなぜ芸術と見なしうるか」、出原均、藁科英也編『菅
　木志雄』展カタログ、広島市現代美術館他を巡回、1997年、p. 15

"Things" and "Sites": The World of Kishio Suga

Akira Tatehata

The statement entitled "Released Scenic Space," published in the catalogue for Kishio Suga's solo exhibition last year, is a noteworthy text that summarizes in the most concise manner the issues related to the "things" (*mono*) and "sites" (*ba*) that the artist has discussed from various perspectives for many years.

> When there are "things," it is necessary to consider that there is also inevitably a "site." The "essence of things" and the "essence of site" are always back-to-back, and cannot be considered separately from one another under any situations. It can be said that when one perceives "things," one also integrates the "site" into one's consciousness. ... Things, so to speak, exist within a "site" as focal points, yet as site by nature is that which is insubstantial, it is not possible to observe it in the same way as things. That being said, as long as the presence of "things" does not disappear, the "site" is undeniably present as an expanse that naturally exists. On the contrary, one could say that things are able to maintain their nature as a result of the presence of "site."[1]

This relationship between "things" and "sites," which take on an insubstantial form, recalls the field theory in physics, where particles do not interact directly with each other, but through fields, if you will forgive my completely amateurish discussion. While the Japanese *ba* is rendered as "site" in the English translation of the aforementioned text, in field theory it translates as "field" in English and "champ" in French. Since the *ba* in Suga's usage is "an expanse that naturally exists," it seems logical to conclude that it encompasses a meaning similar to "field" or "champ," in addition to "site."

In fact, the notion that a "thing" is necessarily contiguous with an invisible "field" that takes on an insubstantial form is a consistent feature of Suga's installation works. In a certain sense, depending on one's point of view, his early text, "Existence Beyond Condition" (1970), already expressed a similar awareness in different terms. For something to "exist beyond condition" is to "understand the shift from an object[thing]'s general state of being to the state of existing at its extreme limit."[2] While it may sound like a Zen meditative question, one interpretation is that it is precisely because "things" are always contiguous with an invisible "field" that we are able to recognize not only that "things" are there, but also entities "there as they should be (in the extreme)."

In his essay "A Territory is Not Closed," written in 1999, Suga discusses the nature of his own installations in more detail using the terms "territoriality" and "surroundings."

> My installations show not only things themselves, but also the territoriality (domain) of those things. This territoriality conforms to the character of the space, but it is more accurate to say that this character is revealed by the things that exist in that territoriality. In the case of a bronze figure, for example, its territoriality is a space that accepts it (including its artificiality). By contrast, the territoriality of a thing in a natural climate such as a stone or tree, becomes a space that these things can inhabit, imbuing the territoriality with distinctive character.[3]

If an installation is neither an expression the spatial arrangement and composition of things nor an expression of environment, but rather "something that shows the things themselves as well as the territoriality in which they exist," then the nature of site and territoriality are undoubtedly deeply overlapping concepts, even if they cannot be considered identical."

Let us examine some concrete examples. Suga's early work *Diagonal Phase* (1969) (cat. no. 2, p. 23), which is on display at this exhibition, is a simple piece in which two rectangular pieces of timber lean on each other at an angle, while two small natural stones are placed at each end where the work touches the floor, as if to sandwich these wooden beams.

The extreme state of a thing, whether it is an everyday object or a work of art, is also a state of namelessness in which no meaning has been assigned.

The combination of wooden beams in *Diagonal Phase* depends on the simple physics of gravity. This installation is only a literal demonstration of a state in which the beams are placed on the floor and lean against each other, including the arrangement of the stones (although the first presentation of the work was outdoors). It has nothing to do with any intent to create a form.

So what kind of territoriality do these "things" of rectangular timber and stones reveal?

In one of his texts from 1997, Suga notes that "I feel it necessary to intentionally understand 'invisible forms' as objects of our consciousness." He elaborates: "When setting up a particular structure, it would not be wrong to think of it as an open space where one's field of vision is not obstructed. In such a situation, if we look at the state of things as a whole, it would not be a mistake to say that the 'visible' and 'invisible' intermingle to create a unified form (territory)." [4]

In a certain sense, this idea represents an early prototype of Suga's theory of "site." "The way things are, and the content of what we perceive, will be different depending on whether we view them from the perspective of a person looking at them as a closed structure or an open space...It seems to me that an open structure is directly connected to the 'surroundings' of a thing. Sometimes it is impossible to make an accurate judgement about where the structure ends and the 'surroundings' begin. In this regard, the way things are in a 'site' or 'territory' and their relationship to each other can then also be thought of in terms of a 'relationship to the surroundings.' This relationship needs to be clearly recognized and organized. In the end, we seem to be unable to fully embody our own thinking through things." [5]

If *Diagonal Phase* had been viewed solely in terms of its visible form, it would have been regarded as a minimalist work from which all expressive elements had been removed. According to Suga, however, it is a "site" or "territory" with an open structure and bears a "relationality to its surroundings" just as it is. Although these two statements were made nearly a quarter of a century apart, they are trying to say almost exactly the same thing: "the 'visible' and 'invisible' intermingle to create a unified form (territory)," and "'thingness' and 'site-ness' are always contingent, and cannot be considered separately from one another under any situations." This stance had already been evident in Suga's early works. In *Diagonal Phase*, wood and stones do not exist in a matter-of-fact way. Rather, they exist as they should in terms of a "relationality to their surroundings." To put it another way, as long as things exist, insubstantial sites and territories will inevitably arise.

Let us now take a look at *Infinite Situation I (window)* (fig. 1), which was created the year after *Diagonal Phase*. This work, which has only been preserved in photographs, was created by opening a window at the National Museum of Modern Art, Kyoto and inserting a thick piece of rectangular timber into the window frame in a slanting position: an artwork left in a state that surely deserves to be called "abandoned."

fig.1　*Infinite Situation I (window),* 1970, Installation view at The National Museum of Modern Art, Kyoto, Japan. Photo: Kishio Suga

In his text *"Being Left* as Situation" (1971), Suga wrote: "What I call *being left* is the idea of taking methodologies or concepts of [thing]s and/or situations that have become incapacitated in our already conceptualized perception of art and setting them outside the present institution of art."[6] "And since at times the eloquence of [thing]s often surpasses human parlance to be more imaginative than even our imaginativeness, I initially had to destroy the imagination the [thing]s themselves had by putting them in a sticky situation. And so it was that I had to leave the [thing]s and their situations there."[7]

It is interesting to note that what Suga calls "being left" is not only a repudiation of the artist's subjective expression, but also a rejection of "the imagination of the *object* itself," which is "more imaginative than human imagination." Objets, beginning with Dada and Surrealism, continue to have a life of their own in contemporary art, even as their forms may shift. For Suga, "being left" is not about scattering or discarding things, but rather the act of abandoning such fetishistic imaginations and directly perceiving the extreme state in which things exist.

The appearance of a rectangular piece of timber inserted into a window frame is not matter-of-fact, mysterious, or even site-specific. Rather, we might say that it has an open structure as a site.

*

Assuming that the dynamics governing the "site" in this sense have nothing to do with formalist principles or fetishism, is this site just a random, anarchic expanse? Naturally, it cannot be such a thing, since it is an unparalleled "territory" that continues to fascinate us deeply.

According to Suga, in his installations, things are scattered in such a way as to exclude centripetal force, with each thing having equal autonomy, and "there is no sense of completeness." "Instead, in an installation, the 'complexity' and 'diversity' contained in the various things that make up the site (surroundings) and are still untouched can be presented in their original form and state."[8]

Since I have discussed Suga's early works so far, I would now like to turn my attention to *The Cultivation of Mother Earth* (cat. no. 87, pp. 74–75), created in 2000. This work consists of five triangular pyramids on the floor, each of which is made of three steel pipes and stands about three meters high. Each of these pipes is anchored in a bucket (except for one, which has a wooden base). There are also several other buckets, some of which have a white rope tied to it. Perhaps this is a misreading, but I would interpret the title as a reference to the creation of a site that is equivalent to nature. This work is not a self-contained space: it contains a "complexity" and "diversity" that make up the site (surroundings), while still possessing the dynamics of generation.

Suga even goes so far as to say that, "It is like pulling on the end of a string and finally getting to know its entire length. Perhaps it is also a natural outcome that the work can be likened to the syntax of words, letters, and sentences. Putting words together and arranging sentences have something in common with installations."[9]

Here, I would like to focus on his use of the

word "syntax." Suga, as we all know, is also an excellent writer. "Even in an installation, when the consciousness of a single human being intervenes, a personal 'worldview' is still involved."[10] The dynamics of a site are not anarchic: a syntax operates within it, just as with letters and sentences. This is true not only of Suga's installations, but also his two-dimensional works and painted reliefs.

*

This may seem somewhat abrupt, but here I would like to bring in the poem "Un coup de dés jamais n'abolira le hasard" ("A throw of the dice will never abolish chance") by the 19th century Symbolist poet Stéphane Mallarmé. Published posthumously, this consummately difficult twenty-one-page poem basically maintains a configuration based on lines but divides them minutely and arranges them using a variety of typefaces in different sizes to form a "constellation" of letters on each double-page spread.

In one of the spreads, Mallarmé writes that *"rien aura eu lieu que le lieu"* ("nothing will have taken place but the place") (fig. 2). If this "place" (or "site") is "nothing other than the formation of the 'page'" (Hidetaka Ishida), then Mallarmé suggests that this page may still constitute an autonomous place or field within the book. What is striking here is how this sentence is divided into three lines, which are discreetly mixed in with the other lines. The stars (letters) that make up these constellations (fields) are telling us, through their own syntax, that words are effectively the creation of fields. (As I mentioned earlier, the French word for site is *champ,* not *lieu,* and this difference may conceal a latent problem related to the concept of a "page" — but I will have to elaborate on this issue on another occasion.)

fig.2 Stéphane Mallarmé, "Un coup de dés jamais n'abolira le hasard," Librairie Gallimard (copyright by Nouvelle Revue Française). July 1914. p. 24.

At any rate, the way in which words and places in "Un coup de dés" are maintained in a state of reciprocity is something that is rather difficult to articulate. To put it somewhat bluntly, "thing-ness" and "site-ness" are always contingent and cannot be considered separately from one another under any situations. It seems to me that this corresponds to Suga's statement that "when we perceive things, the site also enters our consciousness." So when Suga himself says that "putting words together and arranging sentences have something in common with installations,"[11] my observation is not entirely off the mark.

(Incidentally, in terms of the relationship of Suga's works to language, Toshiaki Minemura notes that "as utterances become language when segmented, things become something akin to words when segmented," and "by that, I have meant that he is able to speak the language of things." Minemura's argument that "the segmentation of things leads to the segmentation of space at the same level as things," and that the viewer "thus know[s] that things' transparent words are transformed into a poem of opaque beings,"[12] may shed a different kind of light on this situation.

*

In terms of his relief works, Suga's recent pieces such as *Halted Areas* (2016) (cat. no. 105, p. 92) and *Connected Sites* (2017) (cat. no. 106, p. 92) comprise rectangular forms in various sizes attached to a rectangular board in various orientations, covered entirely in white acrylic paint. While these works might appear to be abstract compositions, the artist's intentions are neutral regarding the composition itself, as indicated by how the words "areas" and "sites" are included in the titles. These works are not self-contained: they are unenclosed areas that are almost synonymous with their surroundings (for Suga, "surroundings" is not a concept based on binary opposition, such as that of center and periphery).

Suga's works did away with the modernism in art (which had lingered on in conceptualism in terms of how the latter rejected figurative expression as a representation of ideas) and opened completely new possibilities. I reserve my deepest esteem for this artist who has eschewed successive shifts in isms and, from his early works to the present, has consistently maintained a position that is entirely his own.

(President, Tama Art University)

Notes

All quotations are by Kishio Suga, except citation 12.

1. "Released Scenic Space" in *Kishio Suga: Released Scenic Space* (Tokyo: Tomio Koyama Gallery, 2020) p. 7
2. "Existence Beyond Condition," (translated by Mika Yoshitake) in *Kishio Suga Writings, Vol. I: 1969–1979* (eds. Andrew Maerkle, Ashley Rawlings, Sen Uesaki, Milan: Skira editore; Los Angeles: Blum & Poe; Sao Paulo, Mendes Wood DM, 2021), p. 134
3. "A Territory Is Not Closed" in *Selected Writings of Kishio Suga: A Territory Is Not Closed* (Yokohama: Yokohama Museum of Art, 1999), p. 11
4. "Bundling Surroundings to Open a Realm's Edges" in *Kishio Suga* (eds. Hitoshi Dehara and Hideya Warashina, Tokyo: Yomiuri Shimbun, 1997), p. 21
5. Ibid, p. 21
6. *"Being Left* as Situation" (translated by Andrew Maerkle) in *Kishio Suga Writings, Vol. I: 1969–1979* (eds. Andrew Maerkle, Ashley Rawlings, Sen Uesaki, Milan: Skira editore; Los Angeles: Blum & Poe; Sao Paulo, Mendes Wood DM, 2021), p. 146
7. Ibid, p. 149
8. "A Territory Is Not Closed," p. 11
9. Ibid, p. 11
10. Ibid, p. 11
11. Ibid, p. 11
12. Toshiaki Minemura, "Why Do We Call It Art?" (translated by Reiko Tomii) in *Kishio Suga* (eds. Hitoshi Dehara and Hideya Warashina, Tokyo: Yomiuri Shimbun, 1997), p. 307. In Tomii's original translation, 分節性 (*bunsetsusei*) is rendered as "articulation." Here, Tatehata has revised the translation to "segmentation" in accordance with its use in Saussurean structuralist linguistics.

The Existence of "Things" and the Eternity of "Site"

KISHIO SUGA

菅木志雄 〈もの〉の存在と〈場〉の永遠

積層空間　Layered Space　1968

斜位相　Diagonal Phase　1969

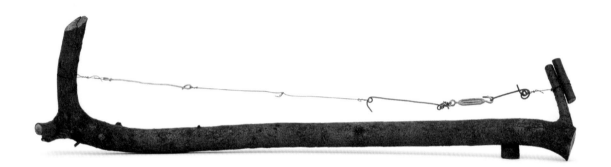

間状帯　Belt of Interstitial Condition　1972

状況体　Bodies of Condition　1973

表間相　Appearance in Phase　1969 / 2012

無為状況　Inactive Environment　1970 / 2012

地因陰律　Territorial Cause, Latent Order　1972 / 2012

水上識体　Floating Units of Perception　1973 / 2012

枝況　Branched Condition　1973 / 2012

木状結律　Law of Wood in Connected State　1973 / 2012

間素　Elements in Space　1973 / 2015

識況　Condition of Perception　1970 / 2006

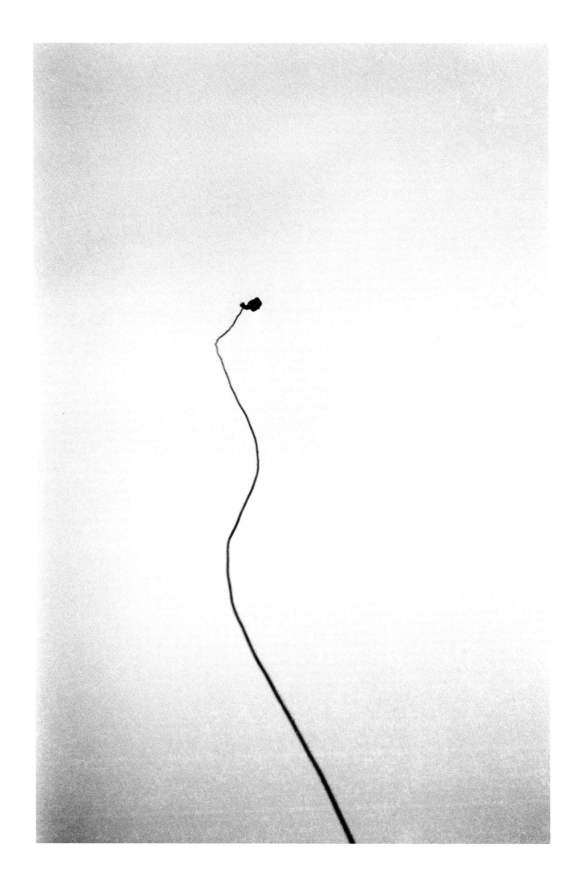

界律 Space-Order 1974 / 2006

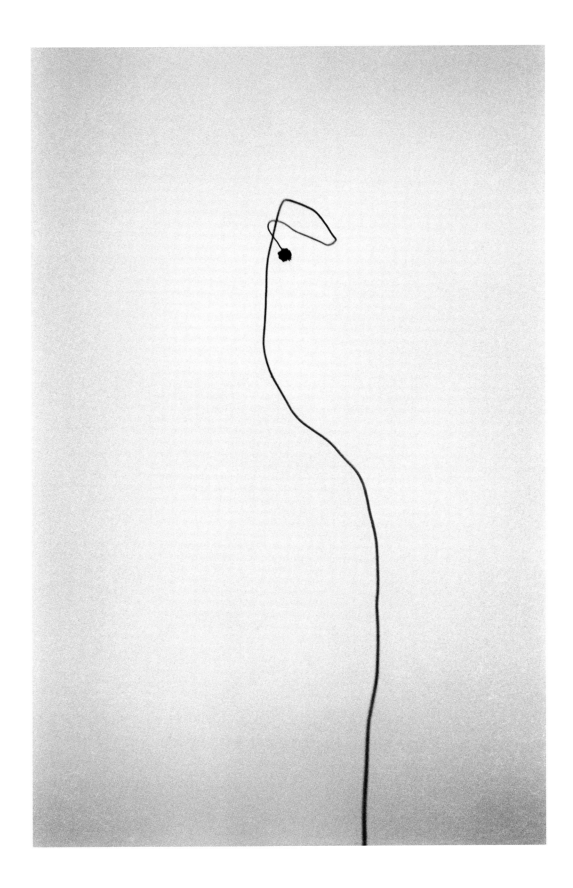

界律 Space-Order 1974 / 2006

等間体　In the State of Equal Dimension　1973 / 2006

依存素　Elements of Dependency　1974 / 2015

無変律　Law of Immutability　1974 / 2015

自然律　Natural Order　1975 / 2012

留地　Fastened Earth　1975 / 2015

留位置　Fastened Placement　1975 / 2012

間留　Remaining Space　1975 / 2012

地動差　Discrepancies of Movement on the Ground　1976 / 2012

界片　Realm of Fragments 1975

依相 175　Phase of Dependence 175　1975

線の界 212　Realm of Lines 212　1974

線の界 211　Realm of Lines 211　1975

線の界 216　Realm of Lines 216　1975

線の界 217　Realm of Lines 217　1975

線の界 217　Realm of Lines 217　1975

線の界 207　Realm of Lines 207　1975

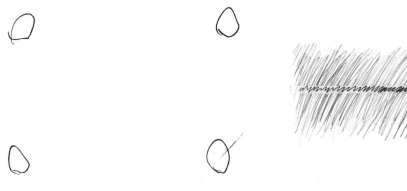

線の界 204　Realm of Lines 204　1976

線の界 205　Realm of Lines 205　1976

線の界 203　Realm of Lines 203　1976

離空　Divergent Space　1975

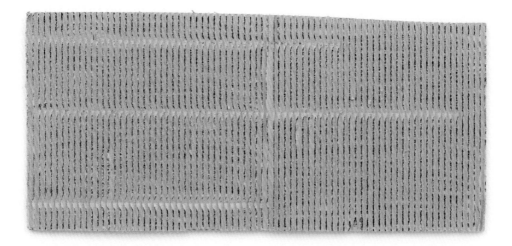

領空 Territorial Void 1978

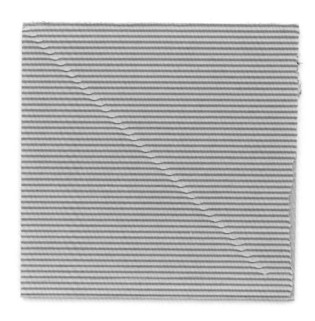

過中 Passing the Interior 1978

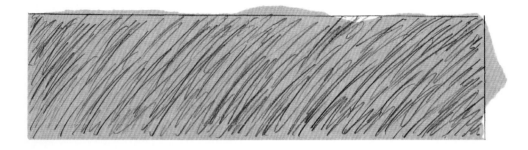

域場　Area of Site　1979

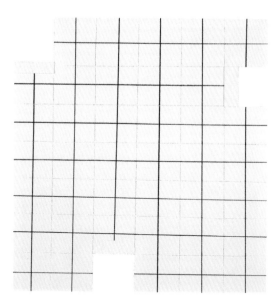

界囲構　Enclosed Space　1980　　　　　　　　　　　　　　　集為論　Theory of Gathering　1980

対空　Confronting Spaces　1980

在置向　Existence of Placed Orientation　1981

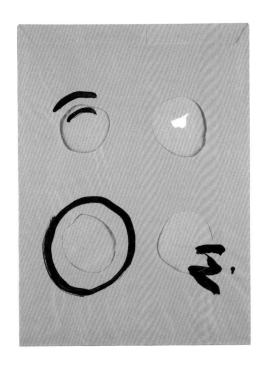

作用空　Effects of Voids　1982

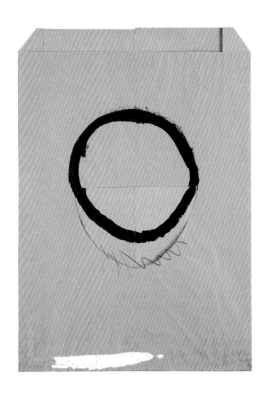

切り取られた分間　Separation of Divided Intervals　1982

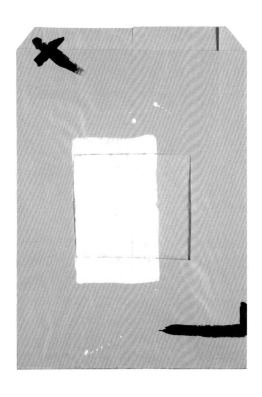

占められた領辺　Occupied Territory and Edges　1982

事位　Matter and Location　1980

AS FACTS−1　1980

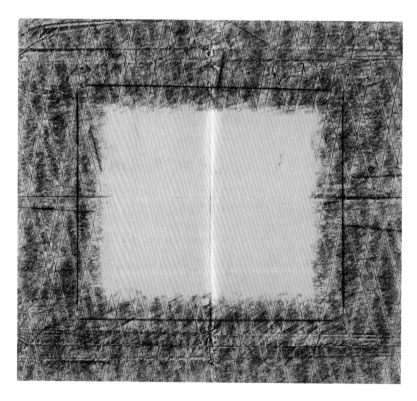

AS FACTS−10　1980

臨界面 081　Surface of Critical Boundary 081　1981

D系列　The Series D　1982

集の支え　Support of Accumulation　1983

内側の作用 No. 4　Effects of Interior No. 4　1985

内側の作用 No. 3　Effects of Interior No. 3　1985

スクエアポンド　Square Pond　1986

縁辺消失　Disappearance of Edges and Sides　1986-1987

わたし自身が、もの の限界をつくりだすのではなく、状況がそのまま、限界のきわまった場所としてあることを見定め、そこにもっとも自然な在り方を措定することである。

1971 年『Kishio Suga 1988–1968』（私家版、1988 年）より

ものの周辺が、中央にあるものの実体性を支えるためだけにあると考えるのは、まちがいである。周辺そのもののリアリティーがなければ、中央にあるもののリアリティー（現実感）が生まれるはずがない。どだい〈中央にあると思われるもの〉も、他のナニカの周辺だからである。

1988 年『Kishio Suga 1988–1968』（私家版、1988 年）より

境界線上に〈もの〉がある。また境界の〈あたり〉でシステムが成立する—という思いがわたしにはある。

1994 年「内側の力、外側の存在」『Japan: Triennale India 1994』（国際交流基金）より

わたしは、たいがいの場合、作品に「秩序」を変えるように要素や構築性を仕くんでいる。あるときは、まったく異なる「秩序」を入れ、ものの見方や思考を刺激し、そこに「別の世界」があるということを知らしめたいと考えるのである。

2005 年「「有」間「無」間」『菅木志雄作品は禅に通じる』（板室温泉 大黒屋 菅木志雄倉庫美術館、2008 年）より

表現されるものは、もともとある〈場〉の構築性と実体性を変えなければ、人の意識を動かすものにならない。人の意識を動かすとは、日常性から少しずれた自然の在り方であり、見慣れない状況性が〈もの〉によって、〈場〉にもたらされたときである。

2015 年「集存の開空」『菅木志雄』（ヴァンジ彫刻庭園美術館）より

モノは、だいたいにおいて、ヒトに無関係な時間を在りつづけている。それはヒトには簡単に理解できないような集積である。たとえ時間をかけたとしても〈在ることのプロセス〉を感知することはむずかしいと思われる。時間の長さも、その在り方もである。

2021 年「集められた〈中間〉」『菅木志雄 集められた〈中間〉』（小山登美夫ギャラリー）より

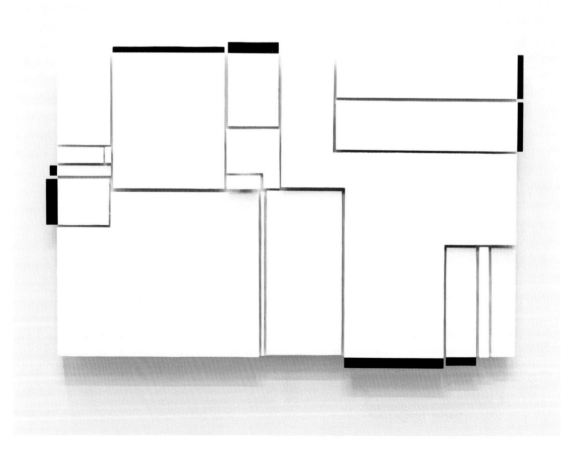

PROTRUSION ZX87 1987

PROTRUSION 000   1987

PROTRUSION HX87   1987

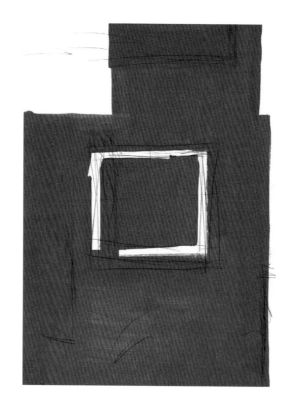

無端　No Edge　1983

無在　No Existence　1983

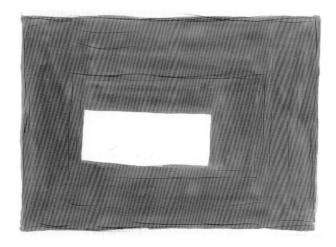

無題　Untitled　1985

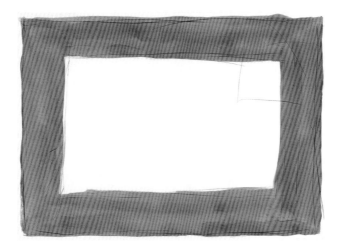

無題　Untitled　1985

無題　Untitled　1985

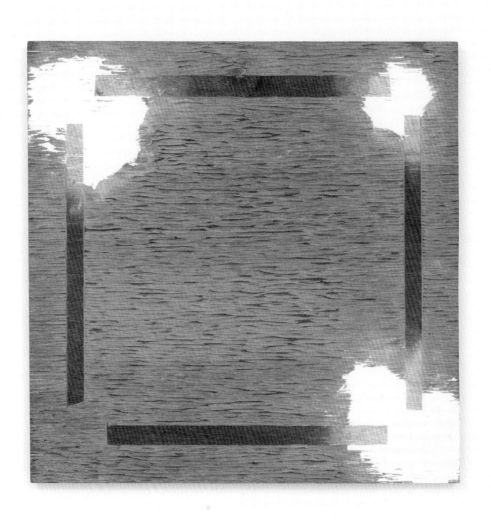

補われた素材-58　Supplemented Material-58　1984

景集素　Scene of Gathered Elements　1984–1991

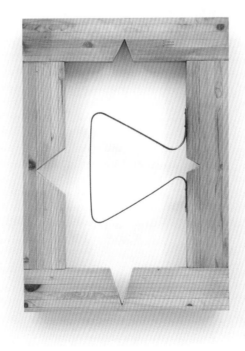

周切囲合　Surrounded Separation and Enclosed Conjunction　1988

上弦・間・下弦・Waxing-Space-Waning 1990

離図周界　Separated Diagram, Surrounding Realm　1990

I do not create the limits of a thing, but rather they are created by the circumstances which determine its optimum position; when existing in its most natural way.

1971 *Kishio Suga 1988–1968*, private press, 1988

To assume that peripheries only exist to assure reality of a central point is wrong. The thing placed in the center cannot have any reality without reality of surrounding things. And even the central point is, in fact, only a periphery to something else.

1988 *Kishio Suga 1988–1968*, private press, 1988

"Something" exists on the borderline. Also, a system formulates "in the neighborhood" of the border. This is an idea that I have.

1994 "External Power—External Presence," *Japan: Triennale India 1994*, The Japan Foundation

When I make artworks, I intentionally put elements and structures that transform orders in the works themselves. This intention goes as far as to input completely different orders that would influence ways of seeing and thinking in viewers, so that the viewer actually believes there could be "another world."

2005 "Between 'being' and 'nothingness'," *Kishio Suga's Work from a Zen Perspective*, Kishio Suga Souko Museum, 2008

Unless that which is expressed changes the constructivity and substantiality of the original "site," it will not turn into something that affects people's consciousness. People's consciousness is affected when a state of nature that is slightly different from the everyday or an unfamiliar situationality is induced in a "site" by "mono."

2015 "The Open Space of Gathered Existing," *Kishio Suga*, Vangi Sculpture Garden Museum

Things, for the most part, continue to be in a passage of time that is unrelated to human beings. It is therefore difficult for humans to easily understand its accumulation. No matter how much time is taken, it seems difficult to perceive the "process of being." This is true both in terms of the length of time, and its very nature.

2021 "Gathered <Intermediates>," *Kishio Suga: Gathered <Intermediates>*, Tomio Koyama Gallery

距離の定位　Determined Position of Distance　1990

永遠のコーナー　Corner of Eternity　1990

木の側界　Lateral Realm of Wood　1990

縁を支える二つの木　Two Trees Supporting the Edges　1990

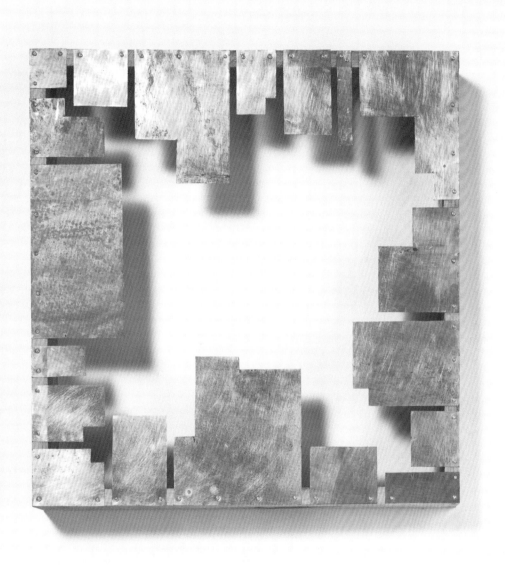

囲間内奥　Surrounded Spaces of Interior Depth　1991

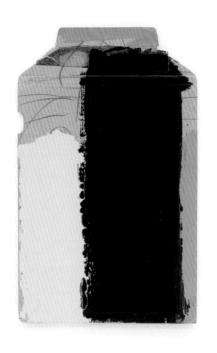

叙々に By Degrees 1990

そこまではいく Go as Far as There 1990

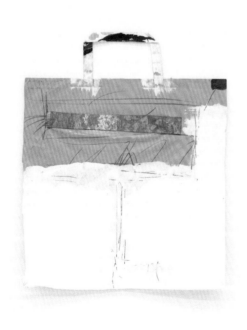

water band 1990

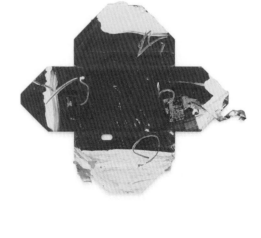

紙構露景 Composition of Paper, Revealed Scenery 1990

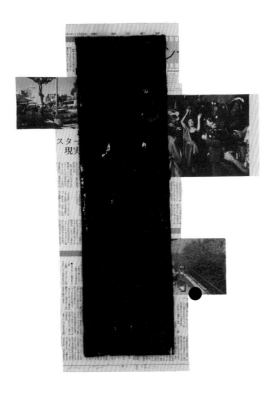

集場（5）　Accumulation of Sites (5)　1992

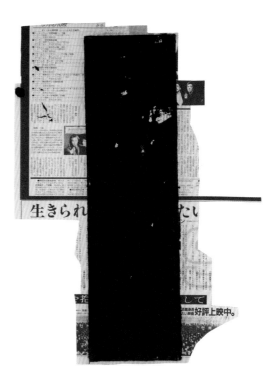

集場（7）　Accumulation of Sites (7)　1992

集場（6）　Accumulation of Sites (6)　1992

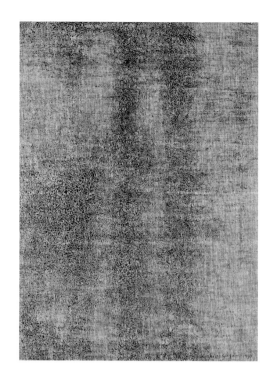

無空　Without Void　1993

無空空　Void Without Void　1993

体の素因　Factors of Body　1993

端の識景　Perceived Scenery of Extremities　1993

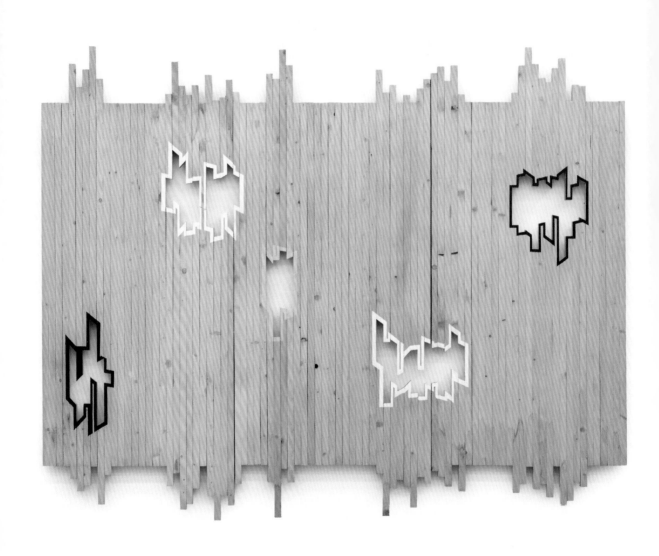

無化景結 Nullification of Scenic Connections 1995

縦横構緑　Composition of Length and Width　1996

周集系　System of Surroundings　1998

大地の育成　The Cultivation of Mother Earth　2000

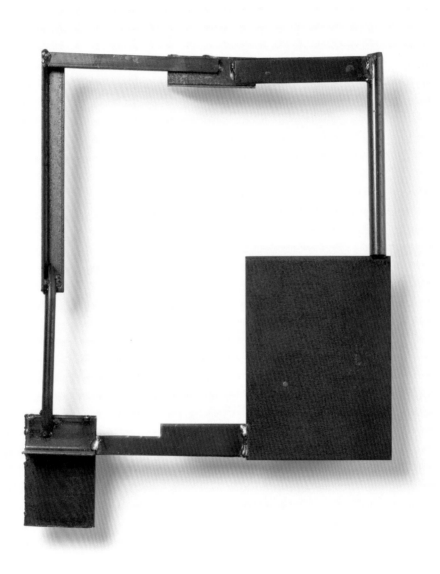

内境然因　Interior Boundaries and Natural Causes　2001

端片移差　Edges of Fragments and Transitional Discrepancies　2001

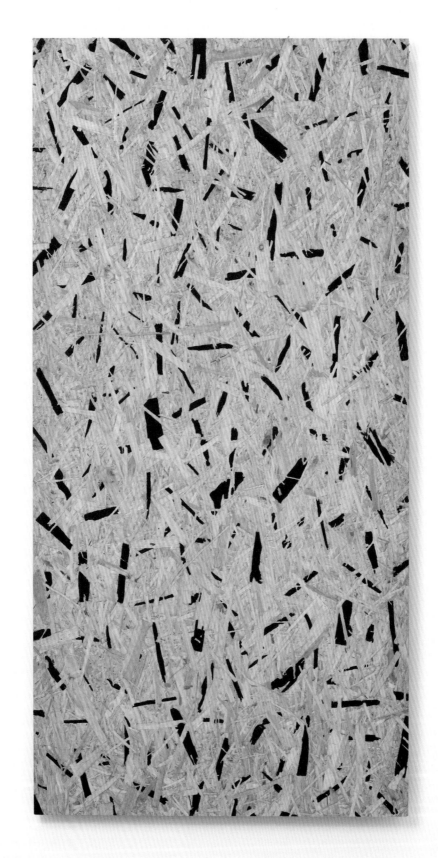

共地　Concurrent Ground　2008

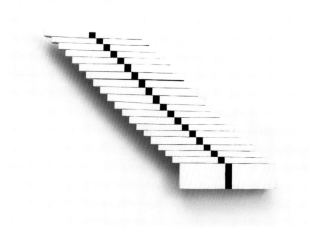

組みかえられた斜向　Recombined Diagonal Orientation　2005

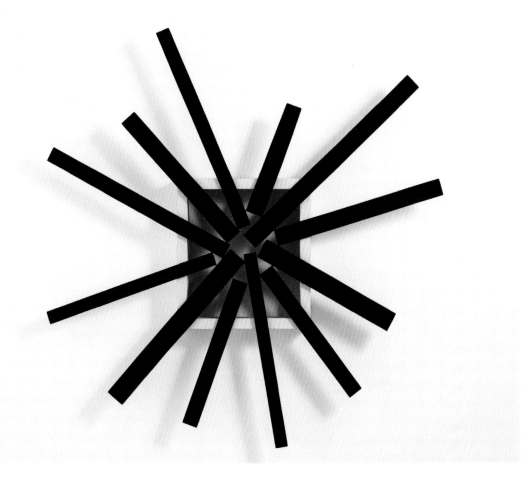

臨中集散　Critical Interior and Gathered Dispersion　2003

揺間　Oscillating Spaces　2005

集向　Gathered Orientations　2005

散立　Dispersed Emergence　2005

対応　Correspondence　2006

複潜化-5　Multiple Latencies in Formation-5　2007

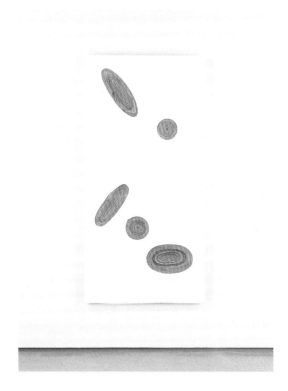

複潜在　Multiple Latencies in Existence　2007

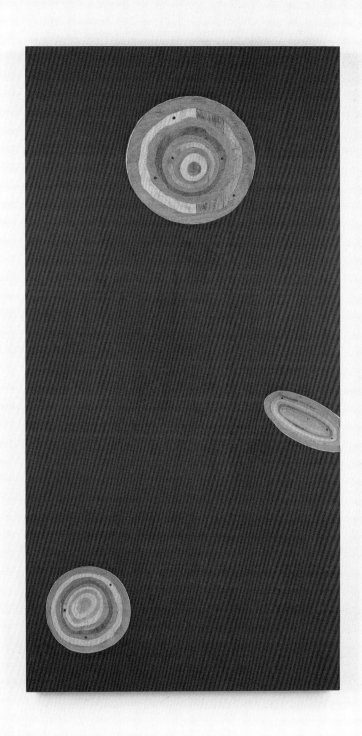

複潜化-6　Multiple Latencies in Formation-6　2007

間を縮める　Shortening the Interstices　2006

間状化　Spacing Situation　2010

連集個　Connecting Surroundings and Individuals　2010–2011

無間静限　Nullification of Intervals and Reposed Limit　2011

空止耕　Halted and Cultivated Space　2017

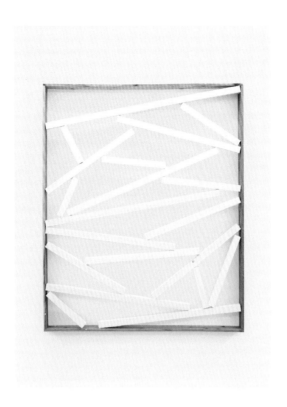

止域　Halted Areas　2016

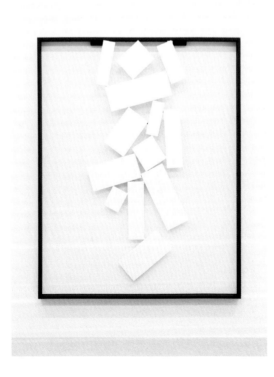

連場　Connected Sites　2017

潜因空 Space of Latent Cause 2017

所成性　Location of Composition　2017

超間　Beyond Space　2018

縁立　Arising Edges　2018

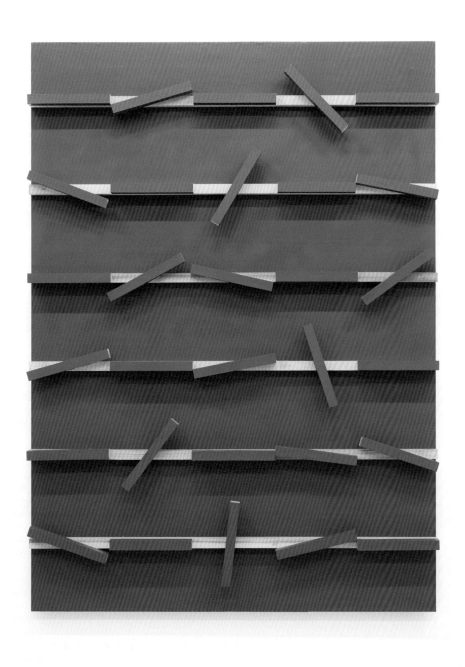

揺化律　Law of Oscillation　2018

深差　Depth of Discrepancies　2019

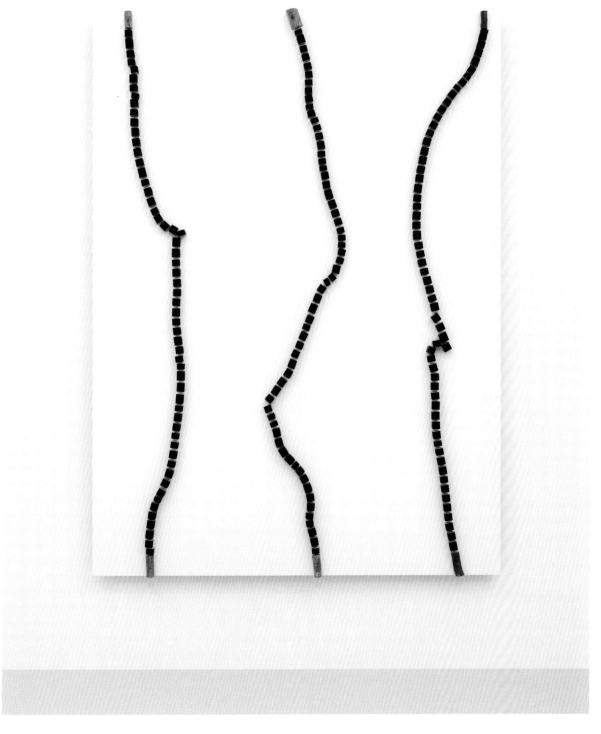

景素　Scene of Elements　2020

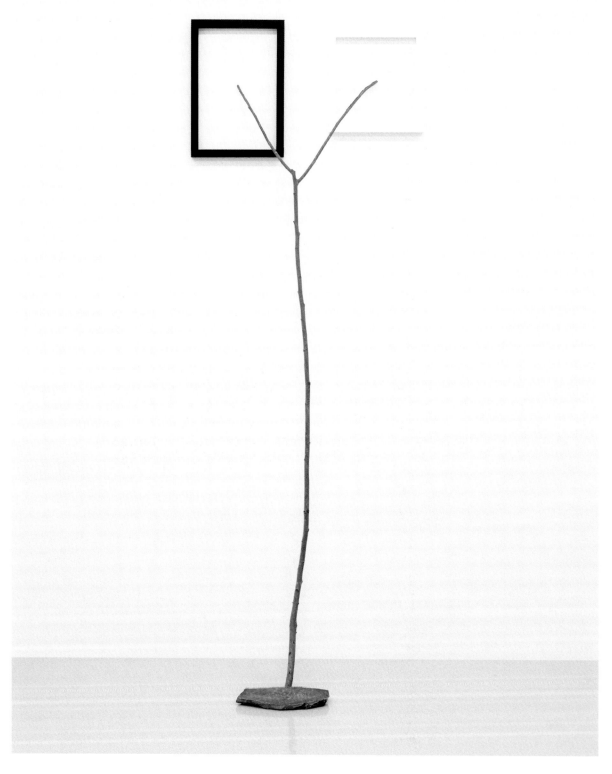

潜深　Latent Depths　2018

菅木志雄と岩手についてのいくつかのこと

濱淵真弓

岩手で生まれ育ち、上京後も70年代から現在まで定期的に岩手で発表を続ける菅木志雄。これまで菅と岩手の関わりをまとめて書き留めた機会は少ないため、ここでは岩手芸術祭と盛岡にある現代美術画廊のギャラリー彩園子（以下、彩園子）での主要な出来事を中心に記し、菅の活動の展開や地元作家との交流を振り返っておきたい。

岩手から上京、1964年に多摩美術大学に進んだ菅は、盛岡出身で後に彩園子オーナーとなる村井睦平（1943–）と知り合う。大学で菅の2年先輩にあたる村井は、関根伸夫と同級で、1967年には関根、吉田克朗らとともに、貸し切った都電で洗濯物を干すハプニング「OOOプラン」にも参加した。卒業後の菅が1969年に田村画廊でパラフィンの板を積み上げた代表作《並列層》を発表したが、村井が会期後にそのパラフィンを譲り受け、翌年に同画廊で巨大なろうそくの形をした作品を発表したという逸話も残っている[1]。

盛岡ではその頃、村上善男らの「集団N39」（1963年結成）、百瀬寿らの「COZMO-8V」（1972年結成）等、既成の美術のシステムに変革を求めたグループが興る。自由な表現を追求する動きは、戦後すぐ創設された岩手芸術祭美術展（以下、芸術祭）にも影響を及ぼし、国内の代表的な現代美術家を招待し特別展示を行うこととなった。そこで選ばれたのが、1970年に第5回ジャパン・アート・フェスティバル大賞を受賞した菅である。こうして、1973年10月、盛岡地区合同庁舎別館[2]にて開催された「状況因」が、郷里での初の個展となった。当時29歳で、前月にパリ青年ビエンナーレ、同月には東京の画廊で展示と、多忙なスケジュールをぬっての制作、発表だった。会場には、松の丸太を針金でつなげた《状況体》（cat. no. 4, p. 25）等計4点が設置されたが、当時の盛岡の人々の目に風変わりに映ったこの展示には「賛否両論が渦巻き、作品の前で小首をかしげる観賞者が相次いだ」[3]。本展への注目により芸術祭には、翌年から「環境芸術部門」（現在の現代美術部門）が立ち上げられることになった。また、菅は1979年から3年にわたり、環境芸術部門の審査員を務めてもいる[4]。

さて、学生時代から付き合いが続いていた村井は1976年に帰郷、1978年に彩園子を開廊した。実家所有の土蔵を、画廊、画材店と喫茶店を兼ねた店舗に改装して開いたものだ。画廊は30平米の空間で、蔵の梁と元あった柱の土台石を床に活かした極めて個性的な空間である。当時の盛岡には何軒かの画廊があったが、現代美術に特化し若い作家たちにも門戸を広げた点で彩園子は画期的であった。

彩園子では、菅の個展が実質の開廊記念展[5]として開催された。花崗岩と、村井宅に残っていた廃材から見つけた柾板（まさいた）を、重ねながら床全体に広げた《辺界》（発表当時は《原状》）（fig. 1）は「ある状況のなかで、ものがどのように依存し合っているか」を提示する機会となった。「この10年間、丸太やコンクリート、自然木といった素材を使って物の在りようを追究してきた菅氏の新しい展開を見せる個展として注目」された[6]。

fig. 1 《辺界》 1978年 撮影：菅木志雄

はじめて彩園子ギャラリーを見に行ったとき、床に土台の石が点々と残って、生活に根ざした空間のあり方が珍しかった。東京あたりの画廊では、決して見かけない生きた空間だった。わたしは、そこで展覧会をしたが、そこほど肩の力を抜いてできる場所はなかった[7]。

彩園子での2回目の展示は1980年のイヴェント《事位》（cat. no. 45, pp. 42-43）であった。これも、村井宅の廃材の板、小枝とともに、画廊のそばを流れる中津川の石を床いっぱいに並べる行為を見せるものであった。本作では、床に埋め込まれた石も作品の一部に取り込まれた。また、ドローイングシリーズ「線の界」（cat. nos. 25-33, pp. 34-35）も2階の喫茶店「一茶寮」で展示している。

　この時は夜に一茶寮で交流会が催され、地元作家の杉本吉武、百瀬寿、小笠原卓雄、藁谷収らが集った。現代美術の最新情報を得る機会の少なかった彼らにとって、菅から聞く東京や世界の美術状況の話はよい刺激になったという（fig. 2）[8]。さらに翌日、テレビ局勤務の杉本の計らいで、菅は情報番組に生出演した。「菅木志雄さんの環境芸術」として、菅がレンガでガラス板を挟んだ小品を制作するイヴェントをスタジオで披露している（fig. 3）[9]。なお、《事位》の略図（fig. 4）は出演前の打合せ時に描いたと杉本は記憶している。

fig. 2　一茶寮での地元作家との交流会（1980年5月）。写真中央から左へ：菅、杉本吉武、藁谷収、小笠原卓雄　撮影：橋本尚恣

fig. 3　岩手放送の情報番組「ラブリーいわて」（1980年5月8日放送）写真撮影：橋本尚恣

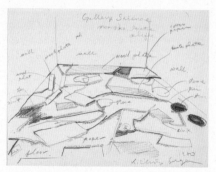
fig. 4　《事位》の略図　1980年

　1982年、菅は3回目の個展で《支行の木》（fig. 5）を発表。材木同士を斜めに立て掛け接点から黒い布を垂直に垂らし、その上に石を置いた作品で、床に広く素材を並べる過去の2点とは異なった展開を見せた。杉本は「画廊の床に埋め込まれた石を見て『まいった。これがあまりにも面白いから、やる必要ないんじゃないか』と菅さんが言っていました。この石を活かし、さらに自分で持ってきた石を置いて意味付けるという発想で、いかなるときも創造空間にしていました」[10]と語る。

　本作は画廊近くの木材屋や雑貨屋で材料をそろえ、村井と設置したもので（fig. 6）、現代美術家の長谷川誠は「何年かに1回、展覧会をしに手ぶらで来て、素材を現地調達。もの派ってかっこいいなと思いました。菅さんと村井さんが〔長谷川の〕自宅裏の商店に買いに来ていた記憶があり、ここで素材を買うんだと、新鮮に感じました。作品だけでなく制作過程も見られて面白かったんです」と回想している[11]。

　2019年までに菅は計16回もの展覧会を彩園子で行った。その間、彩園子では、展示室の増改築が行われている。1994年には展示室が増築され、2室（I・II）の構成となった。隣接する盛岡正食普及会の工場2階に作られた新しい展示室IIは、Iと異なるフラットなスペースであり、菅は1995年の《素格》（I）と《素台》（II）より、それぞれの空間の違いを活かした作品を発表するようになった。さらに、2008年の改装を経て、展示室IはL字型の空間に生まれ変わる。菅はL字型の床の中央に沿って角材を並べた《離空化》（2018年）、紙片を並べた《揺潜》（2019年）を展示。後者は直角に曲がった空間を利用し鑑賞者に発見を促す作品である。

国内外で華々しく活躍する菅は、岩手の作家たちにとって希望の光であり、自らの作品や言葉で、美術のあり様や気づきを示してくれた重要な人物だったが、一方の菅は、長い年月にわたりなぜ岩手で発表を続けたのか。

　思うにその一つは、自らの実践を検証する場としての彩園子があったからだ。「普通のことをしたら生活感に負け」[12]てしまうほどの唯一無二の空間が生む、作家に挑ませる空気、そして作家のどんな表現にも寄り添ってくれるオーナー村井の懐の深さ。両者により、菅は彩園子で実験的な作品を次々と生み、検証し、次への展開を一歩踏み出すことができた。

　そして何より、岩手で発表する理由のもう一つは、自然と初めて向き合い、見つめ、「もの」について思索した場所、創作の原点であったからではないか。菅にとって、表現スタイルとしてでなく、生きるために世界とどう向き合っていくべきかを指し示す「もの派」の制作姿勢、それを育んだ地こそ岩手であった。

野山に出かけていって動植物を観察してばかりの少年でした。人と交わるよりも、田んぼのあぜ道を歩き、ドジョウ、ゲンゴロウ、タニシを見ている方が断然好きでした。なぜ彼らはその形で、そこに存在しているのかを考えていました。自然界に存在する物、つまり『もの』について深く考えるという芸術家・菅木志雄の根幹になっている精神構造が作られました[13]。

（岩手県立美術館上席専門学芸員）

註

1. 対談「斎藤義重と『もの派』の成り立ち 菅木志雄×村井睦平」（岩手県立美術館、2003年2月1日）での村井の発言。
2. 展示施設を兼ねた庁舎として1970年に完成した盛岡地区合同庁舎別館は、芸術祭等の作品発表の場として活用された。
3. 「大家、新鋭がきそう 岩手芸術祭美術部門が開幕」『盛岡タイムス』1973年10月9日、7面
4. 過去の審査員にはもの派の作家の榎倉康二、関根伸夫がいた。
5. 村井によれば、村井の父、弥兵衛の書画を展示した靄々居展が画廊最初の展覧会だったが、菅木志雄展が実質の開廊記念展であった。
6. 「依存し合う 構造を問う 菅木志雄展」『岩手日報』1978年5月17日（夕刊）、2面
7. 菅木志雄「春風飛花」『ギャラリー彩園子 30周年に寄せて 1978–2008』ギャラリー彩園子開廊30周年記念事業実行委員会、2008年、pp. 9–10
8. 現代美術家、小笠原卓雄より聞き取り。
9. 版画家、橋本尚恣より聞き取り。
10. デザイナー、杉本吉武より聞き取り。
11. 長谷川誠より聞き取り。
12. 筆者による作家インタビュー（岩手県立美術館、2005年6月27日）。
13. 森田睦「生老病死の旅路：『もの』とは何か 深く考察 菅木志雄さん」『読売新聞』2018年1月27日（夕刊）、5面

fig. 5 《支行の木》設置の様子（1982年10月）。写真右から：菅、岸伸介、大貫憲一　撮影：橋本尚恣

fig. 6 素材の買い出しの帰り（1982年10月）。写真右から：菅、村井睦平　撮影：橋本尚恣

A Few Things About Kishio Suga and Iwate

Mayumi Hamabuchi

Born and raised in Iwate, Kishio Suga has continued to exhibit his work there regularly from the 1970s to the present, even after moving to Tokyo. Since there have been few opportunities to put Suga's relationship with this region down in writing, in this essay I would like to focus on several major events that occurred at the Iwate Art Festival and Gallery Saiensu, a contemporary art gallery in Morioka, and reflect on how his activities have developed, as well as his interactions with local artists.

After leaving Iwate for Tokyo, Suga enrolled at Tama Art University in 1964, where he met Rikuhei Murai (1943–), a Morioka native who later became the owner of Gallery Saiensu. Murai, who was two years Suga's senior at the university, was a contemporary of Nobuo Sekine. In 1967, Murai participated in the OOO Plan, a happening in which he, Sekine, Katsurō Yoshida, and others hung laundry out to dry on a streetcar that they had chartered. After graduating, Suga exhibited his masterpiece, Parallel Strata, at Tamura Gallery in 1969, consisting of paraffin slabs piled on top of each other. After the exhibition came to an end, Murai took over the paraffin and exhibited a huge candle-shaped work at the same gallery the following year.[1]

Around this time, groups such as Group N39 (formed in 1963 by Yoshio Murakami and others) and COZMO-8V (formed in 1972 by Hisashi Momose and others) began to emerge in Morioka, seeking to revolutionize the established art system. This movement to pursue free artistic expression also influenced the Iwate Art Festival, which had been established immediately after the war. The organizers had decided to invite a leading contemporary Japanese artist to participate in a special showcase, and the artist selected for this was Suga, who had won the Grand Prix at the 5th Japan Art Festival in 1970.

Suga's first solo exhibition in his home region was "Cause of Situation," held at the annex of the Morioka District Joint Government Building[2] in October 1973. Twenty-nine at the time, Suga had taken time out of his busy schedule to create and show these works, having exhibited at the Biennale de Paris the previous month, and an exhibition at a Tokyo gallery the same month. A total of four works were installed at the Morioka exhibition, including Bodies of Condition (cat. no. 4, p. 25), which consisted of pine logs connected by wire, but it was seen as odd and eccentric by the people of Morioka at the time: "the show attracted some controversy, and many viewers looked at the works doubtfully, their heads tilted slightly to one side."[3] The intrigue generated by this exhibition led to the establishment of the Environmental Art Division (now the Contemporary Art Division) the following year. Suga also served as a juror for this Environmental Art Division for three years starting in 1979.[4]

Murai, whom Suga had known since his student days, returned to his hometown in 1976 and opened Gallery Saiensu in 1978 by renovating a warehouse owned by his parents into an art gallery, art supply store, and coffee shop. The gallery is a highly distinctive thirty-square-meter space: the warehouse's wood rafters are preserved in the ceiling and the original columns' foundation stones remain embedded in the floor. While there were several galleries in Morioka at the time, Saiensu was revolutionary in terms of how it specialized in contemporary art and opened its doors to young artists.

In fact, Suga's solo exhibition was held to inaugurate the gallery.[5] His work Parameters of Space (at the time of this presentation, it was called Original State) (fig. 1), which featured blocks of granite and piles of wooden slabs that he had found discarded at Murai's house laid out over the entire floor, provided an opportunity to demonstrate "how things depend on each other in a given situation." According to a journalist, "this solo exhibition was noteworthy for showing new developments in Suga's practice, who has been investigating the nature of things using materials such as logs, concrete, and natural timber for the past ten years."[6]

fig. 1 *Parameters of Space*, 1978. Photo: Kishio Suga

The character of the space was also significant for Suga himself. "When I went to see Gallery Saiensu for the first time, I was struck by the way the space was rooted in daily life, with the scattered foundation stones still visible on the floor — the kind of *living, breathing* space that I would never have seen in a gallery in Tokyo. I was able to have an exhibition there, and there was no other place where I could feel completely at ease."[7]

Suga's second exhibition at Saiensu was the 1980 event *Matter and Location* (cat. no. 45, pp. 42–43), during which he performed the act of arranging stones from the Nakatsu River, which runs next to the gallery, along with discarded wooden slabs and twigs taken from Murai's house across the entire floor. Here, the stones embedded in the floor were also incorporated into the work. A series of drawings called *Realm of Lines* (cat. nos. 25–33, pp. 34–35) was also exhibited at the second-floor coffee shop, Issa-Ryō.

On this occasion, a social gathering was held at Issa-Ryō in the evening, attended by local artists including Yoshitake Sugimoto, Hisashi Momose, Takuo Ogasawara, and Osamu Waragai. For artists like them, who had few opportunities to obtain the latest information on contemporary art, Suga's anecdotes about the art situation in Tokyo and around the world were stimulating and beneficial (fig. 2).[8] The next day, Sugimoto, who worked for a TV station, arranged for Suga to make a live appearance on an informational program. As part of "The Environmental Art of Mr. Kishio Suga," Suga presented an event in the studio where he created a small piece of art by sandwiching a pane of glass between bricks (fig. 3).[9] Sugimoto recalls that he had drawn up the diagram for *Matter and Location* at a meeting held before the live appearance (fig. 4).

In 1982, at his third solo exhibition, Suga presented *Supported Wood* (fig. 5), a work in which boards of timber were made to lean diagonally against each other, with a black cloth hung vertically from where they made contact and tethered to the floor by a stone. According to Sugimoto, when Suga saw the foundational stones embedded in the floor of the gallery, he found them so engaging that he no longer saw the need to show his own work. Sugimoto recounts how Suga had the idea of making the most of those stones: by placing another stone that he had brought with him, he gave them meaning and turned the room into a space that

fig. 2 Social gathering with local artists held at Issa-Ryō (May 1980). Photo from center to left: Suga, Yoshitake Sugimoto, Osamu Waragai, Takuo Ogasawara. Photo: Naotsugu Hashimoto

fig. 3 Informational program "Lovely Iwate," broadcast by IBC (May 8, 1980). Photo: Naotsugu Hashimoto

was constantly creative.[10]

This work was installed together with Murai by gathering materials at a timber shop and a general store near the gallery (fig. 6). Makoto Hasegawa, a contemporary artist, recalls that "they would come once every few years, empty-handed, to procure materials locally for an exhibition. I would think to myself how impressive Mono-ha was. I remember Mr. Suga and Mr. Murai came to the store behind my house to buy materials, and I found it refreshing that they would choose to get them here. It was interesting to see not only their work, but also the production process." [11]

By 2019, Suga had held a total of sixteen exhibitions at Saiensu. During this time, its gallery space had been expanded and remodeled. In 1994, the space was enlarged to create two rooms (I and II). The new Exhibition Room II, built on the second floor above the ground floor factory of the adjacent Morioka Seishoku Fukyukai bread shop, is a flat space,

unlike Exhibition Room I. Suga began to show works that made use of the differences between the two spaces in 1995, starting with *Elemental Status* (I) and *Elemental Base* (II). Following the 2008 renovation, moreover, Exhibition Room I was transformed into an L-shaped space. Here, Suga exhibited *Separated Spaces in Formation* (2018), in which he lined up rectangular pieces of timber along the center of the L-shaped floor, and *Wavering Latency* (2019), in which he arranged pieces of paper on the floor. This latter work encourages viewers to make discoveries by using a space contorted at a right angle.

Suga, who had a brilliant career both in Japan and abroad, was a ray of hope for artists in Iwate, as well as an important figure who showed them the state of art and an awareness of its developments through his works and words. Why then did he continue to exhibit in Iwate for so many years?

One reason, it seems to me, is that Iwate was home to Gallery Saiensu, a place where he could examine the state of his own practice. This one-of-a-kind space — so singular that "if you do anything conventional, you'll be overwhelmed by the sense of its having been lived in" [12] — created an atmosphere that challenged the artists, while the owner, Rikuhei Murai, was so expansive in his open-mindedness that he would rally behind

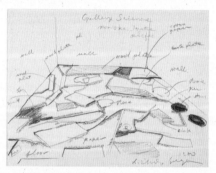

fig. 4 Diagram of *Matter and Location*, 1980

his artists no matter what they produced there. Thanks to these two factors, Suga was able to create a series of experimental works at Saiensu, subject them to scrutiny, and take the next step in his development.

Above all, however, the other reason he chose to present his work in Iwate is that it was where he first came face to face with nature, gazed at it, and contemplated "things" — the starting point of his artistic practice. For Suga, Mono-ha's creative stance, which did not denote a style of artistic expression, but rather indicated how to engage with the world in order to live, had been cultivated by the region of Iwate.

As a boy, I spent most of my time out in the fields and mountains observing plants and animals. I much preferred to walk along the

paths between the rice paddies looking at loaches, dragonflies, and pond snails, rather than interact with people. I would wonder why they existed there, in those forms. The psychological structure that composes the very core of Kishio Suga the artist, who thinks deeply about the things that exist in the natural world — *mono*, in other words — was created there.[13]

(Curator, Iwate Museum of Art)

fig. 5 Installation-in-progress view of *Supported Wood* (October 1982). Photo from right: Suga, Shinsuke Kishi, Kenichi Ōnuki. Photo: Naotsugu Hashimoto

fig. 6 On the way back from buying materials (October 1982). Photo from right: Suga, Rikuhei Murai. Photo: Naotsugu Hashimoto

Notes

1. Murai's remarks from the conversation "Yoshishige Saitō and the Origins of 'Mono-ha': Kishio Suga and Rikuhei Murai" (Iwate Museum of Art, February 1, 2003).
2. The Morioka District Joint Government Building Annex, completed in 1970 as a government office building that also served as an exhibition facility, was used as a venue for exhibiting artworks during art festivals and other events.
3. "Experts and Emerging Talents: Opening of the Art Exhibition of the Iwate Art Festival" in *Morioka Times,* October 9, 1973, p. 7
4. Past jurors include Mono-ha artists Kōji Enokura and Nobuo Sekine.
5. According to Murai, the first exhibition at Saiensu was "Ai-ai-kyo," a show of calligraphy and painting by Murai's father Yahei named for his pseudonym, but it was in fact the Kishio Suga exhibition that formally inaugurated the gallery.
6. "Mutually Dependent, Questioning Structure: Kishio Suga" in *Iwate Nippō,* May 17, 1978 (evening edition), p. 2
7. Kishio Suga, "*Shunpū hika* (Spring Wind, Flying Flowers)" in *30 Years of Gallery Saiensu, 1978–2008,* Gallery Saiensu 30th Anniversary Executive Committee, 2008, pp. 9–10
8. From a conversation with contemporary artist Takuo Ogasawara.
9. From a conversation with print artist Naotsugu Hashimoto.
10. From a conversation with designer Yoshitake Sugimoto.
11. From a conversation with Makoto Hasegawa.
12. From an artist interview by the author (Iwate Museum of Art, June 27, 2005).
13. Mutsumi Morita, "A Journey of Life, Aging, Sickness, and Death: What are 'Mono'? An In-depth Inquiry by Mr. Kishio Suga" in *Yomiuri Shimbun,* January 27, 2018 (evening edition), p. 5

菅木志雄インタビュー

故郷岩手で

— まずは生まれ育った場所についてお教えください。

菅：生まれは盛岡です。2歳から5歳くらいまでは岩泉にいたと思う。それで、近くの龍泉洞によく遊びに行きました。今みたいにきれいになっていなくて、昔の洞窟のような感じでした。ただ、水だけはすごくきれいで、カジカを捕りに行ったもんですよ。
その後が北上。田んぼの真ん中の家で、なぜだか家がブルーでした。そこには小学校1、2年くらいまでいたんじゃないでしょうか。町の感じとしては悪くなかったですよ。
その後、小学校3年くらいで花巻に移って、そこで一番長く過ごしました。花巻小学校、花巻中学、それから高校と、10年くらいいたんです。だから、花巻で生まれて育ったといってもおかしくはないですね。
小さい時から友達はいなくて、自然の中をぶらぶら一人で歩くのが好きでした。虫とか動物とかばかりに付き合って、ほとんど人間はいなかったんです。自然人みたいなもんですね。

盛岡の村井睦平さん

菅：盛岡の因縁といえば、ギャラリー彩園子のオーナー、村井睦平さんです。村井さんとの付き合いは主に大学に入ってからですね。斎藤義重さんの教室に行っているうちに、村井さんとの交流もできました。新宿ピットインで、村井さん、関根伸夫さんらと集まって、やっていましたね。
田村画廊で、村井さんが巨大なろうそくのようなすごいものを作ったんですよね。1969年、僕が田村画廊でパラフィンを使った作品を作ったんです。そういう因縁があります。パラフィンはぐにゃぐにゃしたり固まったり、素材として面白い。そういう素材性の問題に僕は興味があったんです。
村井さんとはとても気が合うし、思考性も合っています。彼も自分の思ってることを曲げないんですよね。自分が思ったら絶対にこれだって言う。僕もそういうタイプだから、お互いの存在を認め合うことが非常に重要だとよくわかりますよ。

— 1970年代に村井さんがギャラリーを始められると聞いた時、どう思われました？

菅：村井さんが「盛岡に帰って、蔵を改造してギャラリーをやる」と言うので「それ、いいね。そういうところがあるんだから、もう東京にいなくていいじゃない」という話をしました。彼もそんなに悪い感じじゃなかったですよ。すごいなあと感心しましたが、どんなもんだろうかと疑問もありました。
その後、実際に行ってみたら、村井さんは大変な地主でした。困るどころかすごいんですよ。大きな蔵を改造して、上は喫茶店にして、下を画廊にして、悠々自適でやっていたんですね。

盛岡での個展

— 1973年には盛岡合庁別館で個展「状況因」を開催。盛岡で初めての個展で、盛岡の人にインパクトを与えた展覧会だったのでは。

菅：そうですかね。変な丸太があるって思われていたんじゃないですかね。

— この翌年に岩手芸術祭の環境芸術部門、今の現代美術部門が立ち上がった。その前段としての、特別展示として発表されたんですよね。
それから1978年には、先ほどの話のとおり、村井さんがギャラリー彩園子を立ち上げられました。菅さんの「辺界」がギャラリーの実質のオープン記念展。

菅：びっくりしたでしょうね。村井さんから何でもいいからやってくれって言われ、僕だって普通の作品はやれないって思いましたよ。いろんな素材を使うことがすでに頭の中にあって、村井さんの倉庫のそばに板切れが放って積んであったんですよ。「これ、使うの？」って聞いたら村井さんは「使わない」。僕が「じゃあ、使いましょう」と。僕の場合には、いかに金をかけずにちゃんと見られるものを作るかが課題でした。これは村井さんのところの材料でうまくいきました。

八幡平の別荘

— 80年代には八幡平に別荘を構えられましたね。

菅：親父が土地を買って放っていたので、友達で建築家の菱沼利行君に頼んで別荘を作ったんです。ちょうど岩手山が真正面に見えて、この場所を大変気に入っています。岩手山っていい山。僕の心の故郷です。ちょっと林の中に入ったら、ニホンカモシカやタヌキ、いろんな動物が出てくるんですね。そういうやつらと付き合ってて、それで人間とは付き合わなかった。僕の気持ちは最高でした。

毎年、夏の間1か月ちょっとくらい行ってました。信長の嫁で、濃姫の若い時の名前が帰蝶というのだけど、帰蝶山荘っていう名前を付けました。

検証の場、ギャラリー彩園子

— 夏を八幡平で過ごして、だいたい秋に彩園子で個展を開く、というサイクルですね。現在までに、彩園子で20回近く展覧会をしていらっしゃいます。

菅：まずは村井さんのところで最初に作品を提示してみて、どういう反応か見ます。「いけそうだな」とか「ここを修正しないとだめだな」と検証して、その上で他に持っていって、やる、という考えでいました。今でもそれはあまり変わりません。

— 彩園子の空間がいいんでしょうね、大きさも雰囲気も。

菅：雰囲気も人間もいいですからね。村井さんと作品を一緒に見て、村井さんが「うーん、いいんじゃない」と一言言うと「いいんだな」と思うんです。それで完成。

宮沢賢治の存在

— 80年代には宮沢賢治の絵本の仕事、90年代には宮沢賢治記念館での企画展「賢治と縄文」に携わっていらっしゃいます。菅さんにとって、宮沢賢治とは特別な存在ですか。

菅：特別というわけでもありませんが、岩手だと宮沢賢治は一大巨匠だから、そこに関われば自然といろんな広がりが出てきます。賢治と自分は、場所的に同じところに立ってる感じがするんです。

花巻の緑ヶ丘に巨大な賢治の石碑が建っています。僕はその近所に住んでいて、そこが毎日の遊び場でした。そして、賢治の「風の又三郎」などをしょっちゅう耳にしたり、読んだりしていました。賢治が畑をやってた頃の家もあり、すごく近いわけです。あまり他人行儀に見てるのではなく、賢治がいた世界の中にいたという感覚がすごく強い。だから、いろんなところで賢治の話が出てくると、僕も賢治が拾った石ころのように、そこにいたんだなと感じました。花巻中学校のすぐそばに、賢治が教えていた花巻農学校があって、行ってみたいなとも思っていましたよ。その風土とか空気とか、何を見てきたかとか。そういったものを体験的に持ってるなという気がしますね。

— 自然観にも影響を受けていますか。

菅：百姓みたいに畑をやってることに、僕は非常に共鳴していますからね。できれば僕も百姓をやりたいと思っていました。当時は釜石に行くのも東京に行くのも蒸気機関車。真っ黒な機関車が煙を吐きながら走ってる。例えば、東京へ行くのに一日掛かるから、一旦乗ったら帰って来られないっていう意識があるんですね。だから、僕はあまり旅行が好きではなく、いやだと思いながら乗ってました。父親が転勤してあちこち動くことが、僕にとってはしんどかった。どうしてもああいうものに乗って行くこと自体の状況性があまり好きじゃなかったんです。

花巻では住んでいた場所がたまたま高校に近かったからよかった。途中、山を分け入って歩いて高校に行っていたのが一番楽しかったんです。僕自身はおそらく文明性に対して非常に近づきがたい、近づけない人間だったんじゃないかなと思っていますよ。ものの発展や発達を嫌悪していた。だから、体を使う分には全然平気ですけど、機械と共存するような意

識は未だに全然ないですね。

炬燵で文学全集

菅：僕の仕事は結局、自分の体力、知力だけが基本ですから、それがなくなったときにはおしまいだろうと思います。そういう意識が芽生えたのは小、中学校のあたりからです。僕は小説が好きで、とにかく朝から晩まで読むのが基本の生活でした。たまたま僕の家には世界文学全集が揃っていて、それを片っ端からずっと読みましたね。北国だから、暖かい炬燵に当たりながら文学全集を読むのが至上の幸せでした。いやだなと思いながら学校に行って、帰ってきたらすぐ読む。しょうがないから学校にも本を持っていって読んでました。家の本を読み終えると、隣近所で日本文学全集を揃えているところに借りに行ったんです。全部借りて、読みました。
子どもの頃の思い出というか、暮らしぶりが土台になって、徐々にものを考えたり作ったりすることになったんだと思います。自然があるところに生まれたっていうのが大きいですよ。

2021年7月7日　静岡県伊東市の作家スタジオにて
聞き手：濱淵真弓（岩手県立美術館）

Interview with Kishio Suga

In His Home Region of Iwate

— To begin, please tell us about the place where you were born and raised.

Suga: I was born in Morioka, and lived in Iwaizumi from about the age of two to five, I think. So I often went to the nearby Ryūsendō Cave to play. It wasn't clean like it is now, it was like an old cave. But the water was so beautifully clear. We used to go there to catch sculpin. After that, we headed to Kitakami. We lived in a house in the middle of rice fields, and for some reason the house was blue. I think I stayed there until I was in first or second grade. It wasn't a bad place to be.

Then, in third grade, we moved to Hanamaki, where I spent the longest time. I was there for about ten years, from Hanamaki Elementary School to Hanamaki Junior High, and then to high school. So it wouldn't be strange to say that I was born and raised in Hanamaki.

I've never had many friends since I was a child, and I liked to wander around in nature alone. I was always drawn to insects and animals: there were almost no other humans around. I lived and breathed nature.

Rikuhei Murai from Morioka

Suga: In terms of my connection to Morioka, I must mention Rikuhei Murai, the owner of Gallery Saiensu. My relationship with Mr. Murai developed mainly after I entered university. I was able to get to know him while attending Yoshishige Saitō's classes. I used to get together with Mr. Murai, Nobuo Sekine, and others at the Pit Inn in Shinjuku, and show work with them. At Tamura Gallery [in 1970], Mr. Murai made a huge candle-like object. In 1969, I made a work using paraffin at the same gallery. That was one of the things that connected us. Paraffin is interesting as a material because it can be both squishy and hard. I was interested in these kinds of issues pertaining to materiality.

Mr. Murai and I are kindred spirits, and we often share the same line of thinking. He doesn't gloss over or hold back his opinions, either. If he thinks something, he will definitely say it. That's also how I function, so I understand how important it can be to acknowledge each other like that.

— What did you think when you heard that he was going to start a gallery in the 1970s?

Suga: Mr. Murai told me he was going back to Morioka to open a gallery in a converted warehouse. I said it was a great idea. Since he had such a place, he wouldn't have to stay in Tokyo anymore. He didn't seem disappointed, either. While I was impressed, I also began to wonder what it would be like.

Later, when I visited, I found out that Mr. Murai was a very serious landowner. He was far from being in trouble — it was an amazing project. He had remodeled a large warehouse, converting the upper floor into a coffee shop and the lower level into an art gallery, and was living in comfort.

Solo Exhibitions in Morioka

— In 1973, you held your solo exhibition "Cause of Situation" at the annex of the Morioka District Joint Government Building. As your first solo exhibition in Morioka, it must have created quite a stir among the locals.

Suga: I wonder if it did. Perhaps everyone just asked themselves what all those strange logs were doing there.

— The following year, the Environmental Art

Division of the Iwate Art Festival, now the Contemporary Art Division, was established. Your work was presented in a special exhibition as a prelude to that. Then in 1978, as you mentioned earlier, Mr. Murai established Gallery Saiensu. Your "Parameters of Space" was in fact the exhibition that inaugurated the gallery.

Suga: People must have been surprised. Mr. Murai asked me to do whatever I wanted, but I figured that I couldn't just do something normal. I had already been toying with the idea of using various materials, and then I found a pile of wooden slabs that had been left next to Mr. Murai's warehouse. I asked him if he was going to do anything with them, and he said no. So I decided to use them. For me, the challenge was how to make something that would stand up to scrutiny without spending a lot of money. And I was able to do this successfully using Mr. Murai's materials.

Summer House in Hachimantai

— You built a summer house in Hachimantai during the 1980s, didn't you?

Suga: My father had bought a piece of land that remained empty, so I asked my architect friend Toshiyuki Hishinuma to build me a summer house there. I really love that place because you can see Mount Iwate right in front of you. It's a great mountain, something like my spiritual home. Once you step into the forest, you find wild goats, *tanuki* raccoons, and many other animals. I would hang out with them instead of people. It was a great feeling for me.
I used to go there every summer for about a month. Nobunaga Oda's wife, Lady Nō, was known as Kichō when she was younger, and we named the place Villa Kichō.

Gallery Saiensu: A Testing Ground

— So it was basically a cycle of spending the summer in Hachimantai and then having a solo exhibition at Gallery Saiensu in the fall. So far, you have held nearly twenty exhibitions at Saiensu.

Suga: The first thing I would do was present my work at Mr. Murai's gallery and see what kind of response I got. This allowed me to verify if it would work, or if I needed to make some changes. Then I would present it somewhere else. Even now, that approach hasn't changed much.

— Gallery Saiensu seems like it would have been ideal, in terms of both its size and atmosphere.

Suga: That's because both the atmosphere and the people are good. When I look at the work with Mr. Murai and he approves, I'll think it's good to go. That's when the work is finished.

Figure of Kenji Miyazawa

— In the 1980s, you worked on Kenji Miyazawa's picture books, and in the 1990s, you were involved in the "Kenji and the Jōmon" exhibition at the Miyazawa Kenji Museum. Is Miyazawa an important figure for you?

Suga: It's not that he's especially important to me, but Miyazawa is one of the great creative masters from Iwate. If you engage with his work, your horizons will naturally expand. I get the sense that he and I occupy a similar position. There is a huge stone monument to Miyazawa in Midorigaoka, in Hanamaki. I lived in that neighborhood, and it was my daily playground. I always heard about and read Miyazawa's stories, like "Kaze no Matasaburō" ("Matasaburō of the Wind"). There was also a house where he had lived when he was working in the fields, so I felt very close to him. I have a strong sense that I inhabited the world where Miyazawa had lived, rather than just gazing at it from a distance. So whenever I heard about him, I felt that I was there, just like the stone that he picked up. Close to Hanamaki Junior High is Hanamaki Agricultural High School where Miyazawa had taught, which I had always wanted to attend. I wanted to see what the climate and air were like, and what he had seen. These are the kinds of things that I have, as experiences.

— Were you also influenced by his views on nature?

Suga: The idea of working the fields like a peasant really resonates with me. I used to think that I would want to be a farmer if I could.
In those days, steam locomotives were the only way to get to Kamaishi and Tokyo. Black locomotives would run on these routes, belching smoke. It took a whole day to get to Tokyo, for example, so there was a sense that once you got on the train, you couldn't come back. That's why I didn't care much for traveling, and used to hate it the whole time I was onboard. The way that my father was transferred from one place to another for his job was hard for me. I really didn't like the entire situation of riding on those things.
In Hanamaki I was lucky because the place where I lived happened to be close to the high school. What I enjoyed most was walking deep into the mountain to get to school. In terms of my relationship to civilized society, I think I was very unapproachable and withdrawn. I found myself quite disgusted by the development and progress of things. That's why I don't mind using my body at all, but still don't have any sense of coexisting with machines.

Reading the Entire Corpus of Literature Under a *Kotatsu*

Suga: Ultimately, my work is based on my own physical and intellectual strength, and I think it would be the end of me if I lost them. It was in elementary and junior high school that I began to be aware of this. I loved reading novels, and my life would basically revolve around reading them from morning till night. I happened to have a complete collection of world literature in my house, and I kept reading these books from cover to cover. Since we lived up north, reading this entire corpus of literature while sitting under a warm *kotatsu* was the happiest thing in the world. I would go to school filled with resentment, and read as soon as I got home. Then I had no choice but to take the books to school with me and read them there. When I had finished the books at home, I went to a neighbor to borrow their complete collection of Japanese literature. I read the entire thing.
I think these childhood memories, or rather the way I lived, became the foundation for me to gradually start thinking about things and creating art. The fact that I was born in a place with nature was a major factor.

Interview by Mayumi Hamabuchi (Iwate Museum of Art), held at the artist's studio in Itō City, Shizuoka Prefecture, on July 7, 2021.

略歴・活動歴

凡例：
・作家、小山登美夫ギャラリー、佐藤毅氏より提供された資料および『Kishio Suga 1988-1968』（菅木志雄・金子多朔・佐藤毅・森司編、私家版、1988年）、『菅木志雄』展カタログ（出原均・藁科英也編、読売新聞社・美術館連絡協議会、1997年）、『菅木志雄 置かれた潜在性』展カタログ（東京都現代美術館編、HeHe、2015年）、『菅木志雄』展カタログ（森啓輔編、ヴァンジ彫刻庭園美術館、2015年）を参照し編集した。
・美術館で開催の一部を除き、原則として「菅木志雄」のみの展名は省略した。

1944　岩手県盛岡市生まれ。幼少期は岩泉町、北上市、花巻市に転居
1964　多摩美術大学絵画科入学（1968年卒業）
1967　第11回シエル美術賞展1等賞（第1席）受賞
1969　『美術手帖』が募集した「芸術評論」に応募し佳作入選
　　　 詩人、小説家の富岡多恵子と結婚
1970　第5回ジャパン・アート・フェスティバル大賞受賞
1982　多摩美術大学の講師となる（1989年まで）
1984　岩手県八幡平市に別荘を設ける（2003年頃まで）
1994　静岡県伊東市にスタジオを設ける
1999　映画『存在と殺人』（監督・脚本）横浜美術館　制作
2000　小説『渡海鳴鳥』講談社　刊行
2008　小説『樹下草怨』東洋経済新報社　刊行
2009　金沢美術工芸大学大学院専任教授となる（2014年まで）
2015　小説『双天のゴライアス』ヴァンジ彫刻庭園美術館　刊行
2016　第57回（2015年度）毎日芸術賞受賞

現在、伊東市を拠点に制作活動を行う

主な個展

2021
「開館20周年記念 菅木志雄展〈もの〉の存在と〈場〉の永遠」岩手県立美術館、岩手
ギャラリー・シーラ、大邱／ギャラリー・シーラ、ソウル、韓国
「集められた〈中間〉」小山登美夫ギャラリー／スパイラルガーデン、東京

2020
「初期作品展」ギャラリー古今、東京
「KISHIO SUGA, SPACE」ギャラリー・シーラ、大邱、韓国
「放たれた景空」小山登美夫ギャラリー／スパイラルガーデン、東京

2019
「〔揺潜〕」「〔走空〕」ギャラリー彩園子 I・II、岩手
「反界結端」イーチ・モダン、台北、台湾
東京画廊＋BTAP、東京
「測られた区体」小山登美夫ギャラリー、東京
ギャラリー・シーラ、大邱、韓国
「"Kishio Suga" presented by The eN arts collection in collaboration with Tomio Koyama Gallery」eN arts、京都

2018
游庵、東京

メンデス・ウッド・DM、サンパウロ、ブラジル
「〔離空化〕」「〔場極〕」ギャラリー彩園子 I・II、岩手
「写真と映像」8/ ART GALLERY/ Tomio Koyama Gallery、東京
「広げられた自空」小山登美夫ギャラリー、東京
「放たれた縁在」THE CLUB、東京
Blum & Poe、ニューヨーク、アメリカ

2017
「新作展」板室温泉大黒屋、栃木
メンデス・ウッド・DM、ブリュッセル、ベルギー
「70年代、80年代の仕事から」渋谷ヒカリエ 8/ CUBE、東京
「分けられた指空性」小山登美夫ギャラリー、東京
東京画廊＋BTAP、北京、中国
Blum & Poe、ロサンゼルス、アメリカ

2016
ディア・チェルシー、ニューヨーク、アメリカ
「Situations」ビレリ・ハンガービコッカ、ミラノ、イタリア
ギャラリー・シーラ、大邱、韓国

2015
「志向する界景」小山登美夫ギャラリー、東京
ブレイン・サザン、ロンドン、イギリス
シェイン・キャンベル・ギャラリー・リンカーン・パーク、シカゴ、アメリカ
「1980年代」ギャラリー古今、東京
8/ ART GALLERY/ Tomio Koyama Gallery、東京
板室温泉大黒屋、栃木
「菅木志雄 置かれた潜在性」東京都現代美術館、東京
Blum & Poe、ニューヨーク、アメリカ

2014
「菅木志雄」ヴァンジ彫刻庭園美術館、静岡
「1970/80年代」ギャラリー古今、東京
「Kishio Suga: Situated Underlying Existence」旧警備館、コルマール、フランス
「新作展」板室温泉大黒屋、栃木

2013
六本木ヒルズ A/D GALLERY、東京

2012
「新作展」板室温泉大黒屋、栃木
Blum & Poe、ロサンゼルス、アメリカ
「潜態の場化」小山登美夫ギャラリー、東京

2011
「来往舎現代藝術展8『菅木志雄展』」慶應義塾大学日吉キャンパス 来往舎ギャラリー、神奈川
「新作展—空間場の耕作—」板室温泉大黒屋、栃木

2010
Space HONGJEE、ソウル／Gallery 604 J&H、釜山、韓国
「2010 新作展」板室温泉大黒屋、栃木
「視線の奥に観えるコト」ギャラリー古今、東京

「在るということ」金沢美術工芸大学アートギャラリー、石川

2009
「新作展」板室温泉大黒屋、栃木
「Le Cose Esistono」マルジーニ・コンテンポラリー・アート、マッサ、イタリア

2008
ダイワファンデーション ジャパン ハウス、ロンドン、イギリス
「新作展」板室温泉大黒屋、栃木
「開廊30周年記念『〔擬空化〕』『〔複潜〕』」ギャラリー彩園子Ⅰ・Ⅱ、岩手
小山登美夫ギャラリー／ TKGエディションズ銀座／ TKG代官山、東京

2007
「新作展」板室温泉大黒屋、栃木

2006
「京橋界隈 平面と立体2006」かねこ・あーとギャラリー、東京
「新作展」板室温泉大黒屋、栃木
小山登美夫ギャラリー、東京
「空気の流路」東京画廊＋BTAP、東京

2005
「揺らぐ体空―菅木志雄インスタレーション―」岩手県立美術館、岩手
ギャラリー彩園子Ⅰ・Ⅱ、岩手
ギャラリー・シーラ、大邱、韓国
「新作展」板室温泉大黒屋、栃木

2004
「〔散合体〕」東京画廊＋BTAP、東京
「1986–1995 レリーフ／平面展」双ギャラリー、東京
「新作展」板室温泉大黒屋、栃木

2003
ギャラリー彩園子Ⅰ、岩手
東京画廊＋BTAP、東京
「〈Gate〉シリーズを中心とした鉄の作品―鉄の小品―」かねこ・あーと
ギャラリー、東京
「新作展」板室温泉大黒屋、栃木

2002
「〔中空構築遠方〕」東京画廊＋BTAP、東京
「〔散体連築〕」ギャラリー彩園子Ⅰ、岩手
「新作展」板室温泉大黒屋、栃木
かねこ・あーとギャラリー、東京

2001
「〔空境線〕」ギャラリー彩園子Ⅰ、岩手
かねこ・あーとギャラリー、東京

2000
かねこ・あーとギャラリー、東京
東京画廊、東京

1999
かねこ・あーとギャラリー、東京
「菅木志雄―スタンス」横浜美術館、神奈川

1998
かねこ・あーとギャラリー、東京
「開廊20周年記念展『〔平地の構素〕』『〔荒地の結素〕』」ギャラリー彩

園子Ⅰ・Ⅱ、岩手
「〔伝境〕」東京画廊、東京
マスダスタジオ、東京
「対話篇―菅木志雄展」山口県立美術館、山口

1997
「菅木志雄」広島市現代美術館、広島；伊丹市立美術館、兵庫；神奈
川県民ホールギャラリー、神奈川；千葉市美術館、千葉へ巡回
「横囲景」かねこ・あーとギャラリー、東京
マスダスタジオ、東京

1996
「〔領域を敷く〕」東京画廊、東京
「集端と境央に沿って 1996」かねこ・あーとギャラリー、東京

1995
「素格と素台」ギャラリー彩園子Ⅰ・Ⅱ、岩手
「モノの未開性と構築性の必然について」かねこ・あーとギャラリー、東京
「『根底への問い』―1970年代の美術― 第7回」村松画廊、東京
「枠状多界」M画廊、栃木
「菅木志雄の表現展」かねこ・あーとギャラリー、東京
「RESTRIZIONE・Sostenere Le cose」東京画廊、東京

1994
「新作展」かねこ・あーとギャラリー、東京
「集景囲端」双ギャラリー、東京

1993
「物・場・依存」ピガ原宿画廊、東京
「新作立体と平面［景間1993］」かねこ・あーとギャラリー、東京
「景間―1993―」日本橋高島屋コンテンポラリーアートコーナー、東京
「端の周界 ’93」牛渕ミュージアム、愛媛
「集間」板室温泉大黒屋、栃木

1992
「端の集界」プラザ・ギャラリー、東京
「差体延空」かねこ・あーとギャラリー／かねこ・あーとGⅡ、東京
「インスタレーション〔景囲周点〕」ギャラリー彩園子、岩手
「〔PROTRUSION〕」東京画廊、東京
「空囲支間 レリーフ作品」双ギャラリー、東京
「’92新作立体および平面から」かねこ・あーとGⅡ 、東京
「空囲支間 インスタレーション的存在体」双ギャラリー、東京

1991
「《天の点景》完成を記念して」板室温泉大黒屋、栃木
「景間」かねこ・あーとGⅠ、東京
「素景にそって」Gallery Art 倉庫、東京
「素景にそって」双ギャラリー、東京
設置「天の点景」板室温泉大黒屋、栃木
「紙の仕事1990（紙片露景）」かねこ・あーとギャラリー、東京

1990
「まなざしの周辺」東高現代美術館、東京
設置「界の切片」藤野町芸術村、神奈川
「新作 立体・平面」かねこ・あーとギャラリー、東京
「上弦・間・下弦」ギャラリー彩園子、岩手
「〔囲界両縁〕」第一会場 東京画廊、東京
「〔体の側縁〕」第二会場 ヒノギャラリー、東京
「周囲界合」双ギャラリー、東京
コンセプトスペースR2、群馬

1989
ハイネケンビレッジ、東京
設置「界の周光」日本ビソー、長崎
「立体と平面 '89」かねこ・あーとギャラリー／かねこ・あーとGI、東京
「ものと行為の接点」近鉄阿倍野店美術画廊、大阪
「景の背立」鎌倉画廊、東京

1988
「集の周囲」ギャラリー彩園子、岩手
「多の周囲の中から」第二会場　かねこ・あーとGI、東京
「周の体」第一会場　かねこ・あーとギャラリー、東京
「思考の周囲」オフ・ギャラリー、ベルリン、ドイツ
「周囲」双ギャラリー、東京

1987
「支える周縁 [立体1987]」かねこ・あーとGI、東京
「〔PROTRUSION〕」東京画廊、東京

1986
「補われた素材 '86」かねこ・あーとギャラリー、東京
「スクウェア・ボンド」鎌倉画廊、東京

1985
「接立体」第二会場　かねこ・あーとGI、東京
「縁の内外」第一会場　かねこ・あーとギャラリー、東京
「メタリック・ボンド」ギャラリー彩園子、岩手
「支空」スー・ギャラリー、大邱、韓国

1984
「補われた素材 新作平面 '84」かねこ・あーとギャラリー、東京
「波行帯」駒井画廊、東京

1983
「集の支え インスタレーション '83」かねこ・あーとギャラリー、東京
「〔接の界〕」東京画廊、東京

1982
「支行の木」ギャラリー彩園子、岩手
「作用」かねこ・あーとギャラリー、東京
「界の仕切り」かねこ・あーとGI、東京
「Installation」ギャルリー・ボードワン・ルボン、パリ、フランス

1981
「『律へ』様々な素材 (II)」かねこ・あーとギャラリー、東京
「〔PROTRUSION〕」東京画廊、東京
「DENOTATION」サトウ画廊、東京
「所依置」ギャラリー檜、東京

1980
「事界」ギャラリールミエール、山形
「平相―事として―」かねこ・あーとギャラリー、東京
「1980/5月展 界の側縁」ギャラリーキタノサーカス、兵庫
「事位」ギャラリー彩園子、岩手
「体律」白樺画廊、東京
「紙材による平面展 (3)」かねこ・あーとギャラリー、東京

1979
「かねこ・あーとギャラリー '79展」かねこ・あーとギャラリー、東京
「〔界入差〕」東京画廊、東京
「律差」ボックスギャラリー、愛知

「集界律」信濃橋画廊、大阪

1978
「木彫平面展」かねこ・あーとギャラリー、東京
「辺界」ギャラリー彩園子、岩手
「中律」村松画廊、東京

1977
「連律」新田村画廊、東京
「状為論〔為相〕」ときわ画廊、東京
「界」ギャラリー・アクムラトリー2、ポズナン、ポーランド

1976
「間状」かねこ・あーとギャラリー、東京
「〔界差〕」真木画廊、東京
「〔連体〕」東京画廊、東京

1975
「紙材による平面展 (2)」かねこ・あーとギャラリー、東京
「取相」真木画廊、東京
「多分律」真木画廊、東京
「紙材による平面展」かねこ・あーとギャラリー、東京
「位況」ときわ画廊、東京

1974
「Show and event 依存位」田村画廊、東京
「― show and event ― Fieldology〈フィールドロジィ〉」galerie 16、京都

1973
「依存差」サトウ画廊、東京
「状況因」盛岡地区合同庁舎別館、岩手
「依存律」田村画廊、東京

1972
「捨置状況」紀伊國屋画廊、東京
「臨界状況」田村画廊、東京

1971
「放置律」サトウ画廊、東京

1970
「ソフト・コンクリート」田村画廊、東京

1969
「並列層」田村画廊、東京

1968
「転移空間」椿近代画廊、東京

主なグループ展

2021
「Days of Inertia」メンデス・ウッド・DM、d'Ouwe Kerke、レトランヘメント、オランダ
「The Still Point ―まわる世界の静止点」kudan house、東京
「At The Luss House: Blum & Poe, Mendes Wood DM and Object & Thing」ジェラルド・ラス邸、ニューヨーク、アメリカ

「Mountains Carrying Suns」Blum & Poe、東京
「多摩美の版画、50年」多摩美術大学美術館、東京

2020
「Artists for New York」ハウザー＆ワース、ニューヨーク、アメリカ
「5,471 miles」Blum & Poe、東京
「古典×現代2020―時空を超える日本のアート」国立新美術館、東京
「小品展」東京画廊＋BTAP、東京
「EnormousBalls」メンデス・ウッド・DM、ブリュッセル、ベルギー
「Toriawase: A Special installation of Modern Japanese Art and Ceramics」アクランド美術館、チャペルヒル、ノースカロライナ、アメリカ
「100 Collective Signatures of Daegu Art Museum」大邱美術館、大邱、韓国
「Alan Charlton, Robert Barry, Kishio Suga, Richard Long」ギャラリー・シーラ、大邱、韓国
「181 Gallery presents work from Blum & Poe」181 Gallery、サンフランシスコ、アメリカ
「コレクション 現代日本の美意識」国立国際美術館、大阪
「Impermanence」テート・モダン（ザ・タンクス）、ロンドン、イギリス

2019
「DECODE／出来事と記録―ポスト工業化社会の美術」埼玉県立近代美術館、埼玉
「LUMINE meets ART AWARD 2018–2019 EXHIBITION」新宿ルミネ、東京
「横浜美術館開館30周年記念 Meet the Collection ―アートと人と、美術館」横浜美術館、神奈川
「百年の編み手たち―流動する日本の近現代美術―」東京都現代美術館、東京
「TRIBUTE to MONO-HA」カーディ・ギャラリー、ロンドン、イギリス
「昭和後期の現代美術 1964–1989」横浜市民ギャラリー、神奈川
「小山登美夫ギャラリー コレクション展 4」8/ ART GALLERY/ Tomio Koyama Gallery、東京

2018
「バブルラップ：『もの派』があって、その後のアートムーブメントはいきなり『スーパーフラット』になっちゃうのだが、その間、つまりバブルの頃って、まだネーミングされてなくて、其処を『バブルラップ』って呼称するといろいろしっくりくると思います。特に陶芸の世界も合体するとわかりやすいので、その辺を村上隆のコレクションを展示したりして考察します。」熊本市現代美術館、熊本
「現代アートの宝箱 OPAM 利岡コレクション」大分県立美術館、大分
「Minimalism: Space. Light. Object」ナショナル・ギャラリー・シンガポール、シンガポール
「2018 西安当代芸術大展」西安美術館、西安、中国
「1968年―激動の時代の芸術」千葉市美術館、千葉；北九州市立美術館分館、福岡；静岡県立美術館、静岡へ巡回
「Surface of Things」鎌倉画廊、神奈川
「Natura Naturans」メンデス・ウッド・DM、ブリュッセル、ベルギー

2017
「態度が形になるとき―安齊重男による日本の70年代美術―」国立国際美術館、大阪
「Japanorama. A new vision on art since 1970」ポンピドゥー・センター・メス、メス、フランス
「陶芸⇄現代美術の関係性ってどうなんだろう？現代美術の系譜に陶芸の文脈も入れ込んで」Kaikai Kiki Gallery、東京
「Who Can Be Strangers? The Art of Mono-ha and Dansaekhwa」Blum & Poe at Adrian Rosenfeld Gallery、サンフランシスコ、アメリカ
「ビバ・アルテ・ビバ：第57回ヴェネツィア・ビエンナーレ」アルセナーレ、ヴェネツィア、イタリア
「Japan House at SP-Arte」シッシロ・マタラッツォ・パビリオン、サンパウロ、ブラジル
「草月創流90周年記念 勅使河原茜と現代アートのコラボレーション」草月会館、東京
「横浜美術館コレクション展 2017年度第一期」横浜美術館、神奈川
小山登美夫ギャラリー、東京

2016
「Karla Black and Kishio Suga: A New Order」スコットランド国立近代美術館、エジンバラ、イギリス
「新・今日の作家展2016」横浜市民ギャラリー、神奈川
「In Between」Bergamin & Gomide、サンパウロ、ブラジル
「コンテンポラリーの出現・日本の前衛美術1950–1970」パソ・インペリアル美術館、リオデジャネイロ、ブラジル
「Utopias / Heterotopias: Wuzhen International Contemporary Art Exhibition」北柵紡績工場跡地／西柵観光地、烏鎮、中国
「ロバート・モリス＆菅木志雄」Blum & Poe、東京

2015
「Breaking through to the actual via the imagination ― Long museum collection show concept by Yuko Hasegawa」龍美術館、上海、中国
「MONO-HA」ムディマ財団、ミラノ、イタリア
「Construction / Destruction」アルマイン・レッチ・ギャラリー、パリ、フランス
「高橋コレクション展 ミラー・ニューロン」東京オペラシティ アートギャラリー、東京

2014
「開館35周年記念 原美術館コレクション展」原美術館、東京
「開館記念展 横浜市民ギャラリークロニクル 1964–2014」横浜市民ギャラリー、神奈川
「開館40周年記念 1974 第2部 1974年―戦後日本美術の転換点」群馬県立近代美術館、群馬
「日本の抽象―その幾何学的側面」東京画廊＋BTAP、東京
「Other Primary Structures」ユダヤ美術館、ニューヨーク、アメリカ
「Erasure: From Conceptualism to Abstraction」オサージュギャラリー／香港城市大学、香港
「マインドフルネス！高橋コレクション展 決定版 2014」名古屋市美術館、愛知
「JAPON」メマック現代アートセンター、メマック、フランス
「コレクション展 2014-I ○△□―美術のなかの幾何学的想像力」広島市現代美術館、広島
「Abstract Drawing」ドローイング・ルーム、ロンドン、イギリス
「記憶 痕跡 分岐―金沢美術工芸大学・大学院教員退官展」金沢21世紀美術館市民ギャラリーA、石川

2013
「連結__展開」国立現代美術館ソウル館、ソウル、韓国
「六本木クロッシング2013展：アウト・オブ・ダウト―来るべき風景のために」森美術館、東京
「高橋コレクション展―マインドフルネス！」霧島アートの森、鹿児島；札幌芸術の森美術館、北海道へ巡回
「Prima Materia」プンタ・デッラ・ドガーナ、ヴェネツィア、イタリア
「2013-I レイヤー 層が生み出す表現」広島市現代美術館、広島
「トリックス・アンド・ヴィジョンからもの派へ」東京画廊＋BTAP、東京
「Re: Quest Japanese Contemporary Art since the 1970's」

ソウル大学校美術館、ソウル、韓国
「Parallel Views: Italian and Japanese Art from the 1950s, 60s and 70s」ウェアハウス、ダラス、アメリカ

2012
「Tokyo 1955–1970: A New Avant-Garde」ニューヨーク近代美術館、ニューヨーク、アメリカ
「日本の70年代 1968–1982」埼玉県立近代美術館、埼玉；広島市現代美術館、広島へ巡回
「Paper Space: Drawing by Sculptors」インマン・ギャラリー、ヒューストン、アメリカ
「Double Vision: Contemporary Art from Japan」モスクワ近代美術館、モスクワ、ロシア；ハイファ美術館、ハイファ、イスラエルへ巡回
「Requiem for the Sun: The Art of Mono-ha」Blum & Poe、ロサンゼルス；グラッドスーン・ギャラリー、ニューヨーク、アメリカへ巡回

2011
「Villa Tokyo」京橋2丁目再開発エリア、東京

2010
「創造と回帰 現代木彫の潮流」北海道立近代美術館、北海道
「MOTコレクション 入り口はこちら—何が見える?」東京都現代美術館、東京
「Contemporary Art of China and Japan」釜山市立美術館、釜山、韓国

2009
「NO MAN'S LAND 創造と破壊＠フランス大使館」在日フランス大使館旧館、東京

2008
「Mediations Biennale」ポズナン国立美術館、ポズナン、ポーランド
「フリーズ・アート・フェア」彫刻公園、ロンドン、イギリス
「アート・バーゼル 39 アート・アンリミテッド」メッセ・バーゼル、バーゼル、スイス

2007
「What Is Mono-ha?」東京画廊+BTAP、北京、中国
「開館記念展 20世紀美術探検—アーティストたちの三つの冒険物語—」国立新美術館、東京

2006
「東野芳明を偲ぶオマージュ展「水はつねに複数で流れる」」ギャラリーTOM、東京
「縄文と現代—二つの時代をつなぐ『かたち』と『こころ』」青森県立美術館、青森
「越後妻有アートトリエンナーレ2006」福武ハウス、新潟

2005
「もの派—再考」国立国際美術館、大阪

2004
「再考：近代日本の絵画 美意識の形成と展開」東京都現代美術館、東京

2002
「Collaboration II—菅木志雄・はやしまりこ」ギャラリー彩園子II、岩手
「未完の世紀—20世紀美術がのこすもの」東京国立近代美術館、東京

2001
「Collaboration—菅木志雄・はやしまりこ」ギャラリー彩園子II、岩手
「Mono-ha（School of Things）」ケトルズ・ヤード・ギャラリー、ケン

ブリッジ；ニューリン・アート・ギャラリー、ニューリン、イギリスへ巡回
「グローバル・ヴィジョン—1980年代から今日まで」東京都現代美術館、東京

2000
「第3回光州ビエンナーレ 日・韓現代美術の断面展」ビエンナーレ館、光州、韓国

1999
「『もの派』二人展—菅木志雄・李禹煥」M画廊、栃木

1998
「アート/生態系 美術表現の『自然』と『制作』」宇都宮美術館、栃木

1997
「重力—戦後美術の座標軸」国立国際美術館、大阪
「超克するかたち—彫刻と立体」千葉市美術館、千葉

1996
「美術の内がわ・外がわ—何故、眼差しは交わったか—」板橋区立美術館、東京
「版画の1970年代」渋谷区立松濤美術館、東京
「コレクションによるテーマ展示：12のインスタレーション」東京都現代美術館、東京

1995
「SOH 10周年展—連鎖— SIX ARTISTS Part 3 菅木志雄＋吉澤美香展 定在と境位」双ギャラリー、東京
「ASIANA contemporary Art from The Far East」パラッツォ・ヴェンドラミン・カレルジ、ヴェネツィア、イタリア
「戦後文化の軌跡 1945–1995」目黒区美術館、東京；広島市現代美術館、広島；兵庫県立近代美術館、兵庫；福岡県立美術館、福岡へ巡回
「1970年—物質と知覚 もの派と根源を問う作家たち」岐阜県美術館、岐阜；広島市現代美術館、広島；北九州市立美術館、福岡；埼玉県立近代美術館、埼玉；サンテティエンヌ近代美術館、サンテティエンヌ、フランスへ巡回

1994
「モノ派 1994 Part III」鎌倉画廊、東京
「素材の領分—素材を見直しはじめた美術・工芸・デザイン」東京国立近代美術館工芸館、東京
「第8回インド・トリエンナーレ」ラリット・カラ・アカデミー、ニューデリー、インド
「戦後日本の前衛美術」横浜美術館、神奈川；グッゲンハイム美術館ソーホー、ニューヨーク；サンフランシスコ近代美術館、サンフランシスコ、アメリカへ巡回
「矩形の森—思考するグリッド」埼玉県立近代美術館、埼玉

1992
「70年代日本の前衛 抗争から内なる葛藤へ」ボローニャ市立近代美術館、ボローニャ、イタリア；世田谷美術館、東京へ巡回

1991
「現代日本美術の動勢—立体造形」富山県立近代美術館、富山
「'70s ～ '80 "モノ派"の作家たち〈PART3〉」鎌倉画廊、東京
「箱の世界—do it yourself—」水戸芸術館現代美術ギャラリー、茨城

1989
「第20回ビエンナーレ・ミデルハイム・ジャパン」ミデルハイム野外彫刻

美術館、アントワープ、ベルギー
「アート・エキサイティング'89 ―現在を超えて― 日豪交換 現代日本美術展」埼玉県立近代美術館、埼玉；クイーンズランド州立美術館、ブリスベン、オーストラリアへ巡回
「創面展」双ギャラリー、東京
「地・間・余白―今日の表現から」埼玉県立近代美術館、埼玉

1988
「11人の作家による 現代美術1988展」何必館京都現代美術館、京都
「色・形・音をめぐっての三週間」双ギャラリー、東京
「Monoha: La scuola delle cose」ローマ大学付属現代美術実験美術館、ローマ、イタリア
「美術史探索學入門 美術館時代が掘り起こした作家達展」目黒区美術館、東京

1987
「第2回JAPAN牛窓国際芸術祭 第2回ビエンナーレ 彫刻と空間」牛窓オリーブ園、瀬戸内、岡山
「現代東北美術の状況展・II」福島県立美術館、福島
「TAMA VIVANT '87 ものからものがたりへ」シブヤ西武シードホール、東京
「もの派とポストもの派の展開 1969年以降の日本の美術」西武美術館、東京

1986
「Japon des Avant-Gardes: 1910–1970」ポンピドゥー・センター、パリ、フランス
「第22回今日の作家'86 現代美術の黙示録（I）魂の深層から」横浜市民ギャラリー、神奈川
「李禹煥・関根伸夫・菅木志雄：70年代の方法」双ギャラリー、東京
「現代の『白と黒』」埼玉県立近代美術館、埼玉
「モノ派 PART II」鎌倉画廊、東京
「Seoul Contemporary Asian Art Show」国立現代美術館、ソウル、韓国
「monologue / dialogue 菅木志雄・狗巻賢二」なびす画廊、東京
「日本現代美術展」台北市立美術館、台北、台湾
「第2回東京野外現代彫刻展」都立砧公園、東京
「空間・素材・表現の新たな展開を求めて」東京日仏学院ギャラリー、東京

1985
「オープニング記念展―現代美術とともに―」双ギャラリー、東京
「第21回今日の作家 '85展 インスタレイションとは何か」横浜市民ギャラリー、神奈川
「第2回アジア美術展」福岡市美術館、福岡
「木の美 絵画と彫刻のあいだ展」北海道立旭川美術館、北海道
「現代美術の40年」東京都美術館、東京
「Construction in Japanese Paper」アル・スュッド、ジュネーヴ、スイス
「Artists' Books」フランクリン・ファーネス・ギャラリー、ニューヨーク、アメリカ
「現代彫刻の歩み―木の造形」神奈川県立県民ホール・ギャラリー、神奈川

1984
「現代美術の動向 III 1970年以降の美術―その国際性と独自性」東京都美術館、東京
「開館記念展第3部 現代東北美術の状況展」福島県立美術館、福島
「第2回富山国際現代美術展 TOYAMA NOW '84」富山県立近代美術館、富山
「ヒューマン・ドキュメンツ '84/'85」東京画廊、東京
「現代絵画の20年―1960～70年代の洋画と新しい『平面』芸術の

動向」群馬県立近代美術館、群馬
「近・現代日本の彫刻」山口県立美術館、山口

1983
「現代日本美術の展望―立体造形展」富山県立美術館、富山
「今・アート最前線」伊勢丹美術館、東京
「現代日本の美術2 風景との出会い展」宮城県美術館、宮城
「収蔵品展―今日の美術＝日本とイギリス」東京都美術館、東京
「木のかたちとエスプリ」埼玉県立近代美術館、埼玉

1982
「昭和57年度多摩美術大学芸術祭 特別展」多摩美術大学新館ギャラリー、東京
「Carnegie International」カーネギー美術館、ピッツバーグ、アメリカ
「第4回 シドニー・ビエンナーレ1982 ヴィデオ・パフォーマンス・セクション パフォーマンス」ニューサウスウェールズ州立美術館、シドニー、オーストラリア
「Arteder '82」ビルバオ国際アート・センター、ビルバオ、スペイン

1981
「日本現代美術展 70年代日本美術の動向」韓国文化藝術振興院美術會館、ソウル、韓国
「開館記念特別展第1部 現代日本の美術」宮城県美術館、宮城
「第16回サンパウロ・ビエンナーレ」パルケ・イビラプエラ、サンパウロ、ブラジル
「菅木志雄 小清水漸 二人展」松村画廊、東京
「パフォーマンス・イン・ビデオ」福岡市美術館、福岡
「第1回 平行芸術展」東京小原流会館、東京
「Yoin: Ideas from Japan made in Australia」ヴィクトリア美術カレッジ、グリフォン・ギャラリー、メルボルン、オーストラリア

1980
「平面絵画―その多様化展」福岡市美術館、福岡
「1980 日本の版画」栃木県立美術館、栃木
「シェル美術賞選抜展」東京セントラル美術館、東京

1979
「今日の作家 '79展」横浜市民ギャラリー、神奈川
「Lisbon International Show '79」ガレリア・デ・ベルム、リスボン、ポルトガル
「菅木志雄 高橋雅之 李禹煥 三人展」駒井画廊、東京

1978
「今日の作家 '78展 表現を仕組む」横浜市民ギャラリー、神奈川
「第38回ヴェネツィア・ビエンナーレ」日本館、ヴェネツィア、イタリア

1977
「今日の作家 '77展 絵画の豊かさ」横浜市民ギャラリー、神奈川
「日米現代美術交換展」80 ラントン・ストリート・ギャラリー、サンフランシスコ、アメリカ；神奈川県民ホールギャラリー、神奈川へ巡回
「03・23・03 ―Projects / Performances / Conferences」コンテンポラリー・アート・インスティチュート、モントリオール、カナダ

1976
「第2回シドニー・ビエンナーレ」ニューサウスウェールズ美術館、シドニー、オーストラリア
「七人のイタリア作家と七人の日本の作家 新しい認識への方法・美術の今日展」イタリア文化会館ホール、東京
「Ima: Now Exhibition」ユーイング・ギャラリー、メルボルン大学付属美術館、メルボルン、オーストラリア

「1976 京都ビエンナーレ〈七名の評論家による現代作家展〉」京都市美術館、京都
「パン・コンセプチュアルズ／汎概念」真木画廊、東京

1975
「東京画廊 '76」東京画廊、東京
「Japanese Contemporary Sculpture」クランブルック美術大学院美術館、ブルームフィールドヒルズ、アメリカ

1974
「第7回現代の造形〈映像表現 '74〉」アート・コアホール、京都
「Materials」ファン・アッベ美術館、アイントホーヘン、オランダ
「Japan Art Exhibition」ルイジアナ美術館、フムレベック、デンマーク；イェーテボリ美術館、イェーテボリ、スウェーデン；ヘニ・オンスタッド美術館、オスロ、ノルウェーへ巡回
「Universe (Cosmos): Image Experiments in Serigraphy by Contemporary Japanese Artists」サンパウロ美術館、サンパウロ、ブラジル
「Japan: Tradition und Gegenwart」デュセルドルフ・クンストハレ、デュッセルドルフ、ドイツ
「吉田克朗＋菅木志雄・プリント展」かねこ・あーとギャラリー、東京

1973
「第8回パリ青年ビエンナーレ」パリ市立近代美術館／パリ国立近代美術館、パリ、フランス
「第8回ジャパン・アート・フェスティバル（国内展示）」東京セントラル美術館、東京；リュブリャナ近代美術館、リュブリャナ、スロベニア；デュセルドルフ・クンストハレ、デュッセルドルフ、ドイツへ巡回

1972
「The 1st Contemporary Japanese Graphics Exhibition」ICA、ロンドン、イギリス
「ベスビオ大作戦 プロジェクト展（日本の部）」南画廊、東京
「第1回ナポリ国際美術展 ベスビオ大作戦」イル・チェントロ・ギャラリー、ナポリ、イタリア

1971
「プリント1972ねん展」シロタ画廊、東京
「第4回現代日本彫刻展　強化プラスチックスによる」宇部市野外彫刻美術館、山口
「第10回 現代日本美術展」東京都美術館、東京

1970
「第5回ジャパン・アート・フェスティバル（日本芸術祭）国内展示」東京国立近代美術館、東京；グッゲンハイム美術館、ニューヨーク、アメリカへ巡回
「今日の作家 '70年展」横浜市民ギャラリー、神奈川
「現代美術の一断面」東京国立近代美術館、東京
「第9回現代美術の動向」京都国立近代美術館、京都

1968
「THE 9 VISIONAL POINTS 9つの視点」村松画廊、東京
「00Xてん TAMA FINE ART COLLEGE 00X CLASS」村松画廊、東京

1967
「OOOPLAN」村松画廊、東京
「ユニヴァーシアード東京大会芸術展示」伊勢丹百貨店、東京
「第11回シエル美術賞展」白木屋、東京；京都市美術館、京都へ巡回
「N・S・S展」椿近代画廊、東京

「OOOプラン 午前零時のための8つのイヴェント」新宿ピットイン、東京
「第4回国際青年美術家展 日本・アメリカ展」西武百貨店・SSSホール、東京

主なアクティヴェイション

＊2004年3月に「イヴェント」を「アクティヴェイション」に改名

2017
「定有偏無」横浜美術館、神奈川

2016
「分空」横浜市民ギャラリー、神奈川
「景中回空」ピレリ・ハンガービコッカ、ミラノ、イタリア

2015
「多の潜景」東京都現代美術館、東京

2014
「散間集行」ヴァンジ彫刻庭園美術館、静岡

2009
「庭づくりによるアクティヴェイション 風の耕路」板室温泉大黒屋、栃木

2008
「縁界性」板室温泉大黒屋、栃木
「複潜現化」メッセ・バーゼル、バーゼル、スイス

2006
「複項系」福武ハウス、新潟
「複因様立」板室温泉大黒屋、栃木
「共時対応」小山登美夫ギャラリー、東京

2005
「分有揺化」岩手県立美術館、岩手

2004
「空間の端」横浜美術館、神奈川

1998
「複雑性の点在」千葉市美術館、千葉
「定立と不立へ」神奈川県民ホールギャラリー、神奈川
「野展」山口県立美術館、山口
「離合定位－視間性」伊丹市立美術館、兵庫

1997
「集散－囲束」広島市現代美術館、広島

1995
北九州市立美術館、福岡
「多様性の配分」広島市現代美術館、広島

1990
「縁の間に沿って」東高現代美術館、東京
「周囲構築－910」コンセプトスペースR2、群馬

1987
「EXTEND 多摩美術大学創立50周年記念イベントTAMABIVENTS」

スタジオ200、東京

1986
「露路空ー接点は深い」横浜市民ギャラリー、神奈川

1984
「縁辺は動く」富山県立近代美術館、富山

1981
福岡市美術館、福岡
「Place Continuity」井の頭公園、東京
「SHEbbING」PARCO、東京

1980
「移される個の全体」ギャラリールミエール、山形
「界の行」かねこ・あーとギャラリー、東京
「事位」ギャラリー彩園子、岩手
「事間」かねこ・あーとギャラリー、東京

1979
横浜市民ギャラリー、神奈川

1978
「臨状移体」多摩美術大学八王子校舎グラウンド、東京
日本館、ヴェネツィア、イタリア

1977
井の頭公園、東京
「状為論〔為相〕」常磐公園、東京
「地為論」真木画廊、東京

1976
「動差ーつながりゆく界」イタリア文化会館ホール、東京
「地と知とー距離の集位」国際基督教大学、東京
「そこーそれぞれの位置に」真木画廊、東京
「隅の辺によせて」京都市美術館、京都
「満たされゆく相」真木画廊、東京

1975
「取相」真木画廊、東京
「間の集積」真木画廊、東京
「自然律」常磐公園、東京

1974
「依存位」田村画廊、東京
「Fieldology」galerie 16、京都

1973
「依存律」田村画廊、東京
「並観ー自在体」作家アトリエ、東京

主な野展

1977
「空律」井の頭公園、東京

1974
「流位在、無変律、周位、界律、界位、依存素、素界、位界依、界在、

周依」よみうりランド／多摩川、神奈川

1973
「等間体」井の頭公園、東京
「界体」井の頭公園、東京

1972
「野展」上州屋ビル屋上、東京
「状況置」作家アトリエ、東京

1971
「間の状況」井の頭公園、東京

1969
「到立消点」若林、東京
「斜位相」富士見町アトリエ、神奈川
「表位相」若林、東京

1968
「積層空間」作家アトリエ、神奈川

アクティヴェイション「多の潜景」
2015年3月7日、東京都現代美術館（「菅木志雄 置かれた潜在性」にて）
68分、デジタルデータ
映像撮影：佐藤毅、小山登美夫ギャラリー
映像提供：佐藤毅
画像撮影：佐藤毅

イヴェント「界の行」
1980年9月29日、かねこ・あーとギャラリー（「平相―事として―」にて）
41分、デジタルデータ変換
映像撮影：ビデオインフォメーションセンター
©VICI映像提供：慶応義塾大学アート・センター
画像撮影：金子多朔

アクティヴェイション「分有揺化」
2005年9月3日、岩手県立美術館（「揺らぐ体空―菅木志雄インスタレーション―」
にて）
71分、デジタルデータ変換
映像撮影：岩手県立美術館
画像撮影：佐藤毅

イヴェント「臨状移体」
1978年11月2日、多摩美術大学八王子校舎グラウンド
39分、デジタルデータ変換
映像撮影：菅靖彦
映像提供：小山登美夫ギャラリー
画像撮影：安齊重男

イヴェント「周囲構築−910」
1990年1月28日、コンセプトスペースR2
41分、デジタルデータ変換
映像撮影：佐藤毅
映像提供：小山登美夫ギャラリー
画像撮影：佐藤毅

Biography / Chronology

Note:
This biography / chronology is based on information provided by
the artist, Tomio Koyama Gallery, Tsuyoshi Satoh and reference
to the following publications: *Kishio Suga 1988–1968* (eds. Kishio
Suga, Tasaku Kaneko, Tsuyoshi Satoh, Tsukasa Mori, Private
Press, 1988), *Kishio Suga* (eds. Hitoshi Dehara and Hideya
Warashina, The Yomiuri Shimbun / The Japan Association of Art
Museums, 1997), *Kishio Suga: Situated Latency* (ed. Museum
of Contemporary Art Tokyo, HeHe, 2015) and *Kishio Suga* (ed.
Keisuke Mori, Vangi Sculpture Garden Museum, 2015).

1944	Born in Morioka, Iwate, Japan
	Moves from Iwaizumi to Kitakami and Hanamaki during his childhood
1964	Enters the Department of Oil Painting at Tama Art University, Tokyo (graduates in 1968)
1967	Receives First Prize, The 11th Shell Art Award
1969	Publishes an award-winning essay in *Bijutsu Techō* magazine
	Marries poet and novelist Taeko Tomioka
1970	Receives the Grand Prix at The 5th Japan Art Festival
1982	Lectures at Tama Art University (through 1989)
1984	Builds a vacation home at Hachimantai, Iwate (occupied until around 2003)
1994	Relocates his studio to Tōtari, Itō City, Shizuoka
1999	Writes and directs the screenplay *Existence and Homicide* (Yokohama Museum of Art, Yokohama, Kanagawa, Japan)
2000	Publishes the novel *Across the Sea, Birds Cry* (Kodansha, Japan)
2008	Publishes the novel *Grass and Resentment Beneath the Tree* (Toyo Keizai Inc., Japan)
2009	Appointed Associate Professor at Kanazawa College of Art (through 2014)
2015	Publishes the novel *Goliath of Twin Skies* (Vangi Sculpture Garden Museum, Nagaizumi, Shizuoka, Japan)
2016	Receives the 57th Mainichi Art Award

Lives and works in Itō City, Shizuoka, Japan

Selected Solo Exhibitions

2021
"20th Anniversary of the Iwate Museum of Art: Kishio Suga: The
Existence of 'Things' and the Eternity of 'Site'" Iwate Museum
of Art, Morioka, Iwate, Japan
Gallery Shilla, Daegu / Gallery Shilla, Seaul, South Korea
"Gathered <Intermediates>" Tomio Koyama Gallery / Spiral Garden,
Tokyo, Japan

2020
Gallery Cocon, Tokyo, Japan
"Kishio Suga, Space" Gallery Shilla, Daegu, South Korea

"Released Scenic Space" Tomio Koyama Gallery / Spiral Garden,
Tokyo, Japan

2019
"[Wavering Latency]," "[Flowing Spaces]" Gallery Saiensu I/II,
Morioka, Iwate, Japan
"Suga Kishio: Opposed Realm and Connected Edges" Each
Modern, Taipei, Taiwan
Tokyo Gallery+BTAP, Tokyo, Japan
"Measured Divisional Entities" Tomio Koyama Gallery, Tokyo,
Japan
Gallery Shilla, Daegu, South Korea
"'Kishio Suga' presented by The eN arts collection in
collaboration with Tomio Koyama Gallery" eN arts, Kyoto, Japan

2018
yu-un, Tokyo, Japan
Mendes Wood DM, Sao Paulo, Brazil
"[Separated Spaces in Formation]," "[Place of Extremities]"
Gallery Saiensu I/II, Morioka, Iwate, Japan
"Kishio Suga: Photographs and Videos" 8/ ART GALLERY/
Tomio Koyama Gallery, Tokyo, Japan
"Expanded Self-Space" Tomio Koyama Gallery, Tokyo, Japan
"Released Existence on Edges" THE CLUB, Tokyo, Japan
Blum & Poe, New York, USA

2017
"New Works" Itamuro Onsen Daikokuya, Nasushiobara, Tochigi,
Japan
Mendes Wood DM, Brussels, Belgium
"Work from the 1970s and 1980s" Shibuya Hikarie 8/ CUBE, Tokyo,
Japan
"Divided Orientation of Space" Tomio Koyama Gallery, Tokyo,
Japan
Tokyo Gallery+BTAP, Beijing, China
Blum & Poe, Los Angeles, USA

2016
Dia: Chelsea, New York, USA
"Situations" Pirelli HangarBicocca, Milan, Italy
Gallery Shilla, Daegu, South Korea

2015
"Intentional Scenic Space" Tomio Koyama Gallery, Tokyo, Japan
Blain|Southern, London, UK
Shane Campbell Gallery Lincoln Park, Chicago, USA
"Kishio Suga 1980's" Gallery Cocon, Tokyo, Japan
8/ ART GALLERY/ Tomio Koyama Gallery, Tokyo, Japan
Itamuro Onsen Daikokuya, Nasushiobara, Tochigi, Japan
"Kishio Suga: Situated Latency" Museum of Contemporary Art
Tokyo, Tokyo, Japan
Blum & Poe, New York, USA

2014
"Kishio Suga" Vangi Sculpture Garden Museum, Nagaizumi,
Shizuoka, Japan

"1970s / 80s" Gallery Cocon, Tokyo, Japan
"Kishio Suga: Situated Underlying Existence" Corps de Garde, Colmar, France
"New Works" Itamuro Onsen Daikokuya, Nasushiobara, Tochigi, Japan

2013
Roppongi Hills A/D GALLERY, Tokyo, Japan

2012
"New Works" Itamuro Onsen Daikokuya, Nasushiobara, Tochigi, Japan
Blum & Poe, Los Angeles, USA
"Placement of the Hidden Currents" Tomio Koyama Gallery, Tokyo, Japan

2011
"Kishio Suga" Raiosha Gallery, Keio University Hiyoshi Campus, Yokohama, Kanagawa, Japan
"New Works: Cultivation of Space and Site" Itamuro Onsen Daikokuya, Nasushiobara, Tochigi, Japan

2010
"Kishio Suga" Space Hongjee, Seoul / Gallery 604 J&H, Busan, South Korea
"New Works" Itamuro Onsen Daikokuya, Nasushiobara, Tochigi, Japan
"What One Perceives in the Depth of One's Line of Sight" Gallery Cocon, Tokyo, Japan
"Existence" The Art Gallery, Kanazawa Collage of Art, Kanazawa, Ishikawa, Japan

2009
"New Works" Itamuro Onsen Daikokuya, Nasushiobara, Tochigi, Japan
"Le Cose Esistono" Margini Arte Contemporanea, Massa, Italy

2008
Daiwa Foundation Japan House, London, UK
"New Works" Itamuro Onsen Daikokuya, Nasushiobara, Tochigi, Japan
"'[Doubtful Spaces in Formation],' '[Multiple Latencies],' The 30th Anniversary of Gallery Saiensu" Gallery Saiensu I/II, Morioka, Iwate, Japan
Tomio Koyama Gallery / TKG Editions Ginza / TKG Daikanyama, Tokyo, Japan

2007
"New Works" Itamuro Onsen Daikokuya, Nasushiobara, Tochigi, Japan

2006
"Two Dimension and Three Dimension 2006" Kaneko Art Gallery, Tokyo, Japan
"New Works" Itamuro Onsen Daikokuya, Nasushiobara, Tochigi, Japan
Tomio Koyama Gallery, Tokyo, Japan
"Airflow" Tokyo Gallery+BTAP, Tokyo, Japan

2005
"Uncertain Void: Installation by Kishio Suga" Iwate Museum of Art, Morioka, Iwate, Japan
Gallery Saiensu I/II, Morioka, Iwate, Japan

Gallery Shilla, Daegu, South Korea
"New Works" Itamuro Onsen Daikokuya, Nasushiobara, Tochigi, Japan

2004
"[Dispersed Combination]" Tokyo Gallery+BTAP, Tokyo, Japan
"1986–1995 Relief / Two Dimension" Soh Gallery, Tokyo, Japan
"New Works" Itamuro Onsen Daikokuya, Nasushiobara, Tochigi, Japan

2003
Gallery Saiensu I, Morioka, Iwate, Japan
Tokyo Gallery+BTAP, Tokyo, Japan
"Gate" Kaneko Art Gallery, Tokyo, Japan
"New Works" Itamuro Onsen Daikokuya, Nasushiobara, Tochigi, Japan

2002
"[Distant-Hollow-Construction]" Tokyo Gallery+BTAP, Tokyo, Japan
"[Dispersed Bodies, Connected Constructions]" Gallery Saiensu I, Morioka, Iwate, Japan
"New Works" Itamuro Onsen Daikokuya, Nasushiobara, Tochigi, Japan
Kaneko Art Gallery, Tokyo, Japan

2001
"[Spatial Boundaries]" Gallery Saiensu I, Morioka, Iwate, Japan
Kaneko Art Gallery, Tokyo, Japan

2000
Kaneko Art Gallery, Tokyo, Japan
Tokyo Gallery, Tokyo, Japan

1999
Kaneko Art Gallery, Tokyo, Japan
"Kishio Suga: Stance" Yokohama Museum of Art, Yokohama, Kanagawa, Japan

1998
Kaneko Art Gallery, Tokyo, Japan
"'[Constructed Elements of Level Ground],' '[Fastened Elements of Rough Ground],' The 20th Anniversary of Gallery Saiensu" Gallery Saiensu I/II, Morioka, Iwate, Japan
"[Relayed Boundaries]" Tokyo Gallery, Tokyo, Japan
Masuda Studio, Tokyo, Japan
"Dialogue: Kishio Suga" Yamaguchi Prefectural Museum of Art, Yamaguchi, Japan

1997
"Kishio Suga" Hiroshima City Museum of Contemporary Art, Hiroshima, Japan
[traveled to Itami City Museum of Art, Itami, Hyogo; Kanagawa Prefecture Gallery, Yokohama, Kanagawa; Chiba City Museum of Art, Chiba, Japan]
"Laterally Enclosed Scenery" Kaneko Art Gallery, Tokyo, Japan
Masuda Studio, Tokyo, Japan

1996
"[Disseminating Territory]" Tokyo Gallery, Tokyo, Japan
"Along Gathered Edge and a Centered Boundary" Kaneko Art Gallery, Tokyo, Japan

1995
"Elemental Status and Elemental Base" Gallery Saiensu I/II, Morioka, Iwate, Japan
"On Primitivism of Objects and Inevitability of Construction" Kaneko Art Gallery, Tokyo, Japan
"A Question for Foundation: Art in 70's: The 7th Exhibition" Muramatsu Gallery, Tokyo, Japan
"Framed State, Multiple Realms" M Gallery, Ashikaga, Tochigi, Japan
"Expression of Kishio Suga" Kanaeko Art Gallery, Tokyo, Japan
"RESTRIZIONE: Sostenere le cose" Tokyo Gallery, Tokyo, Japan

1994
"New Works" Kaneko Art Gallery, Tokyo, Japan
"Gathered Scenery, Surrounded Edges" Soh Gallery, Tokyo, Japan

1993
"Thing, Site, Dependency" Piga Harajuku Gallery, Tokyo, Japan
"Scenic Intervals 1993" Kaneko Art Gallery, Tokyo, Japan
"Scenic Intervals —1993—" Contemporary Art Space, Takashimaya Nihombashi Store, Tokyo, Japan
"Edges of a Peripheral Realm" Ushibuchi Museum, Toon, Ehime, Japan
"Gathered Dimensions" Itamuro Onsen Daikokuya, Nasushiobara, Tochigi, Japan

1992
"Edges of a Peripheral Realm" Plaza Gallery, Tokyo, Japan
"Differentiated and Extended Voids" Kaneko Art Gallery / Kaneko Art G2, Tokyo, Japan
"Installation 'Scenic Enclosure of Surrounding Points'" Gallery Saiensu, Morioka, Iwate, Japan
"[PROTRUSION]" Tokyo Gallery, Tokyo, Japan
"Surrounded Space—Supported Dimension, Relief Works" Soh Gallery, Tokyo, Japan
"New Works '92" Kaneko Art G2, Tokyo, Japan
"Surrounded Space—Supported Dimension" Soh Gallery, Tokyo, Japan

1991
"Inauguration of the Permanent Installation 'Point-scape of the Sky'" Itamuro Onsen Daikokuya, Nasushiobara, Tochigi, Japan
"Intervals of Scenery" Kaneko Art G1, Tokyo, Japan
"Along the Elemental Scenery" Gallery Art Soko, Tokyo, Japan
"Along the Elemental Scenery" Soh Gallery, Tokyo Japan
Permanent Installation "Point-scape of the Sky" Itamuro Onsen Daikokuya, Nasushiobara, Tochigi, Japan
"A Piece of Paper Reveals Scenery" Kaneko Art Gallery, Tokyo, Japan

1990
"Peripheral Field" Touko Museum of Contemporary Art, Tokyo, Japan
Permanent Installation "Fragments of Space" Fujino Art Village, Sagamihara, Kanagawa, Japan
"New Works: Paintings, Sculptures" Kaneko Art Gallery, Tokyo, Japan
"Waxing-Space-Waning" Gallery Saiensu, Morioka, Iwate, Japan
"Both Edges of an Enclosed Realm" Tokyo Gallery, Tokyo, Japan
"Edges of Body" Hino Gallery, Tokyo, Japan
"Around Circumstance" Soh Gallery, Tokyo, Japan
Concept Space R2, Shibukawa, Gunma, Japan

1989
Heineken Village Gallery, Tokyo, Japan
Permanent Installation "Space of Surrounding Light" Nihon Bisoh Co. Ltd., Nagasaki, Japan
"Two Dimensions and Three Dimensions" Kaneko Art Gallery / Kaneko Art G1, Tokyo, Japan
"A Contact Point of Action and Objects" Kintetsu Department Store, Abeno, Osaka, Japan
"Scenery of Defiant Stature" Kamakura Gallery, Tokyo, Japan

1988
"Gathered Surroundings" Gallery Saiensu, Morioka, Iwate, Japan
"Out of Multiple Surroundings" Kaneko Art G1, Tokyo, Japan
"Circumference of Body" Kaneko Art Gallery, Tokyo, Japan
"Surroundings of Thought" Off Gallery, Berlin, Germany
"Surroundings" Soh Gallery, Tokyo, Japan

1987
"Supportive Peripheries" Kaneko Art G1, Tokyo, Japan
"[PROTRUSION]" Tokyo Gallery, Tokyo, Japan

1986
"Supplemented Material '86" Kaneko Art Gallery, Tokyo, Japan
"Square Pond" Kamakura Gallery, Tokyo, Japan

1985
"Conjoined Bodies" Kaneko Art G1, Tokyo, Japan
"Border of Interior and Exterior" Kaneko Art Gallery, Tokyo, Japan
"Metallic Pond" Gallery Saiensu, Morioka, Iwate, Japan
"Supporting a Void" Soo Gallery, Deagu, South Korea

1984
"Supplemented Material" Kaneko Art Gallery, Tokyo, Japan
"A Belt of Waves in Progression" Komai Gallery, Tokyo, Japan

1983
"Support of Accumulation '83" Kaneko Art Gallery, Tokyo, Japan
"[Conjoined Realms]" Tokyo Gallery, Tokyo, Japan

1982
"Supported Wood" Gallery Saiensu, Morioka, Iwate, Japan
"Effect" Kaneko Art Gallery, Tokyo, Japan
"Partitioned Spaces" Kaneko Art G1, Tokyo, Japan
"Installation" Galerie Baudoin Lebon, Paris, France

1981
"Towards Order" Kaneko Art Gallery, Tokyo, Japan
"[PROTRUSION]" Tokyo Gallery, Tokyo, Japan
"DENOTATION" Satou Gallery, Tokyo, Japan
"Dependent Placements" Gallery Hinoki, Tokyo, Japan

1980
"Realm of Matter" Gallery Lumiere, Yamagata, Japan
"Flattened Phase: In Terms of Phenomena" Kaneko Art Gallery, Tokyo, Japan
"Periphery of Space" Gallery Kitano Circus, Kobe, Hyogo, Japan
"Matter and Location" Gallery Saiensu, Morioka, Iwate, Japan
"Order of Entities" Shirakaba Gallery, Tokyo, Japan
"Paper Works 3: As Facts" Kaneko Art Gallery, Tokyo, Japan

1979
"'79" Kaneko Art Gallery, Tokyo, Japan
"[Gap of the Entrance to the Space]" Tokyo Gallery, Tokyo, Japan

"Differentiated Order" Box Gallery, Nagoya, Aichi, Japan
"Law of Gathered Space" Shinanobashi Gallery, Osaka, Japan

1978
"Wooden Works" Kaneko Art Gallery, Tokyo, Japan
"Parameters of Space" Gallery Saiensu, Morioka, Iwate, Japan
"Neutral Order" Muramatsu Gallery, Tokyo, Japan

1977
"Continuous Existence" Shin Tamura Gallery, Tokyo, Japan
"Theory of Emerging Situation" Tokiwa Gallery, Tokyo, Japan
"Space" Galeria Akumulatory 2, Poznan, Poland

1976
"Interstitial State" Kaneko Art Gallery, Tokyo, Japan
"[Spatial Discrepancy]" Maki Gallery, Tokyo, Japan
"[Continuous Process]" Tokyo Gallery, Tokyo, Japan

1975
"Paper Works 2" Kaneko Art Gallery, Tokyo, Japan
"Phase of Acquisition" Maki Gallery, Tokyo, Japan
"Law of Multitude" Maki Gallery, Tokyo, Japan
"Paper Works" Kaneko Art Gallery, Tokyo, Japan
"Condition of Situated Units" Tokiwa Gallery, Tokyo, Japan

1974
"Show and event: Units of Dependency" Tamura Gallery, Tokyo,
Japan
"—show and event—Fieldology" galerie 16, Kyoto, Japan

1973
"Separating Dependence" Satou Gallery, Tokyo, Japan
"Cause of Situation" Annex of the Morioka District Joint
Government Building, Morioka, Iwate, Japan
"Law of Dependence" Tamura Gallery, Tokyo, Japan

1972
"Left-Behind Situation" Kinokuniya Gallery, Tokyo, Japan
"Condition of a Critical Boundary" Tamura Gallery, Tokyo, Japan

1971
"Abandoned Order" Satou Gallery, Tokyo, Japan

1970
"Soft Concrete" Tamura Gallery, Tokyo, Japan

1969
"Parallel Strata" Tamura Gallery, Tokyo, Japan

1968
"Space Transformation" Tsubaki Kindai Gallery, Tokyo, Japan

Selected Group Exhibitions

2021
"Days of Inertia" Mendes Wood DM, d'Ouwe Kerke,
Retranchement, the Netherlands
"The Still Point" kudan house, Tokyo, Japan
"At The Luss House: Blum & Poe, Mendes Wood DM and
Object & Thing" The Gerald Luss House, Ossining, New York, USA

"Mountains Carrying Suns" Blum & Poe, Tokyo, Japan
"Fifty Years of Printmaking at Tama Art University" Tama Art
University, Tokyo, Japan

2020
"Artists for New York" Hauser & Wirth, New York, USA
"5,471 miles" Blum & Poe, Tokyo, Japan
"Timeless Conversations 2020: Voices from Japanese Art of
the Past and Present" The National Art Center, Tokyo, Tokyo,
Japan
"Small Works" Tokyo Gallery+BTAP, Tokyo, Japan
"EnormousBalls" Mendes Woods DM, Brussels, Belgium
"Toriawase: A Special Installation of Modern Japanese Art
and Ceramics" Ackland Art Museum, The University of North
Carolina at Chapel Hill, North Carolina, USA
"100 Collective Signatures of Daegu Art Museum" Daegu Art
Museum, Daegu, South Korea
"Alan Charlton, Robert Barry, Kishio Suga, Richard Long"
Gallery Shilla, Seoul, South Korea
"181 Gallery presents work from Blum & Poe" 181 Gallery, San
Francisco, USA
"Collection: The Aesthetics of Contemporary Japan" National
Museum of Art, Osaka, Osaka, Japan
"Impermanence" Tate Modern (The Tanks), London, UK

2019
"DECODE: Events & Records: Post-Industrial Art" The Museum
of Modern Art, Saitama, Saitama, Japan
"LUMINE meets ART AWARD 2018–2019 EXHIBITION" LUMINE
Shinjuku, Tokyo, Japan
"30th Anniversary of the Yokohama Museum of Art: Meet the
Collection" Yokohama Museum of Art, Yokohama, Kanagawa,
Japan
"Weavers of Worlds: A Century of Flux in Japanese Modern /
Contemporary Art" Museum of Contemporary Art Tokyo, Tokyo,
Japan
"Tribute to Mono-ha" Cardi Gallery, London, UK
"Contemporary Art in the Late Showa 1964–1989" Yokohama
Civic Art Gallery, Yokohama, Kanagawa, Japan
"Tomio Koyama Gallery: Works from the Gallery Artists and the
Collection 4" 8/ ART GALLERY/ Tomio Koyama Gallery, Tokyo,
Japan

2018
"Bubblewrap: After Mono-ha, the next established art movement
is Superflat, but that means the interim period overlapping the
years of Japan's economic bubble has yet to be named, and
I think calling it 'Bubblewrap' suits it well. It especially makes
sense if you incorporate the realm of ceramics. This show will
contemplate this period through works including those from
Takashi Murakami's collection." Contemporary Art Museum
Kumamoto, Kumamoto, Japan
"Treasure box of Contemporary Art" Oita Prefectural Art Museum,
Oita, Japan
"Minimalism: Space. Light. Object" National Gallery Singapore,
Singapore
"Beyond the Wall: Xi'an Contemporary Art Exhibition 2018"
Xi'an Art Museum, Xi'an, China
"1968: Art in the Turbulent Age" Chiba City Museum of Art,
Chiba, Japan
[traveled to Kitakyushu Municipal Museum of Art, Riverwalk
Gallery, Kitakyushu, Fukuoka; Shizuoka Prefectural Museum of
Art, Shizuoka, Japan]

"Surface of Things" Kamakura Gallery, Kamakura, Kanagawa,
Japan
"Natura Naturans" Mendes Wood DM, Brussels, Belgium

2017
"Japanese Art of the 1970s through the Photography of Anzaï
Shigeo" The National Museum of Art, Osaka, Japan
"Japanorama. A new vision on art since 1970" Centre
Pompidou-Metz, Metz, France
"What Is the Relationship Between Ceramics and Contemporary
Art? (Considering the Context of Ceramics in the Lineage of
Contemporary Art)" Kaikai Kiki Gallery, Tokyo, Japan
"Who Can Be Strangers? The Art of Mono-ha and Dansaekhwa"
Blum & Poe at Adrian Rosenfeld Gallery, San Francisco, USA
"Viva Arte Viva: The 57th Venice Biennale" Venice, Italy
"Japan House at SP-Arte" Ciccillo Matarazzo Pavillion, Sao
Paulo, Brazil
"Sogetsu 90th Anniversary: Collaboration between Akane
Teshigawara and Modern Art" Sogetsu Kaikan, Tokyo, Japan
"The Exhibition of the Yokohama Museum of Art: Collection 2017
Part 1" Yokohama Museum of Art, Yokohama, Kanagawa, Japan
Tomio Koyama Gallery, Tokyo, Japan

2016
"Karla Black and Kishio Suga: A New Order" Scottish National
Gallery of Modern Art, Edinburgh, UK
"New 'Artists Today' Exhibition 2016: Spaces of Creation:
Mono-ha to the Art of Today" Yokohama Civic Art Gallery,
Yokohama, Kanagawa, Japan
"In Between" Bergamin & Gomide, Sao Paulo, Brazil
"The Emergence of the Contemporary: Avant-Garde Art in
Japan 1950–1970" Imperial Palace, Rio de Janeiro, Brazil
"Utopias / Heterotopias: Wuzhen International Contemporary
Art Exhibition" North Silk Factory / West Scenic Zone, Wuzhen,
China
"Robert Morris & Kishio Suga" Blum & Poe, Tokyo, Japan

2015
"Breaking through to the actual via the imagination: Long
Museum collection show concept by Yuko Hasegawa" Long
Museum, Shanghai, China
"Mono-ha" Fondazione Mudima, Milan, Italy
"Construction / Destruction" Almine Rech Gallery, Paris, France
"Takahashi Collection: Mirror Neuron" Tokyo Opera City Art
Gallery, Tokyo, Japan

2014
"The Hara Museum Collection at 35" Hara Museum of
Contemporary Art, Tokyo, Japan
"Opening Special Exihibition: Chronicle 1964–2014" Yokohama
Civic Art Gallery, Yokohama, Kanagawa, Japan
"1974, Turning Point of Postwar Japanese Art" The Museum of
Modern Art, Takasaki, Gunma, Japan
"Geometric Perspective on Japanese Abstraction" Tokyo
Gallery+BTAP, Tokyo, Japan
"Other Primary Structures" The Jewish Museum, New York,
USA
"Erasure: From Conceptualism to Abstraction" Osage Gallery /
City University of Hong Kong, Hong Kong
"Takahashi Collection 2014: Mindfulness!" Nagoya City Art
Museum, Nagoya, Aichi, Japan
"Japon" Centre d'art contemporain, Meymac, France
"2014-1 Imaginative Geometry" Hiroshima City Museum of

Contemporary Art, Hiroshima, Japan
"Abstract Drawing" Drawing Room, London, UK
"Kioku Konseki Bunki" People's Gallery A, 21st Century
Museum of Contemporary Art, Kanazawa, Kanazawa, Ishikawa,
Japan

2013
"Connecting_Unfolding" National Museum of Modern and
Contemporary Art, Seoul, Seoul, South Korea
"Roppongi Crossing 2013: Out of Doubt" Mori Art Museum,
Tokyo, Japan
"Takahashi Collection: Mindfulness!" Kirishima Open-Air
Museum, Yusui, Kagoshima, Japan
[traveled to Sapporo Art Museum, Sapporo, Hokkaido, Japan]
"Prima Materia" Punta della Dogana, Venice, Italy
"2013-1: Layers of Artistic Expression" Hiroshima City Museum
of Contemporary Art, Hiroshima, Japan
"Tricks and Vision to Mono-ha" Tokyo Gallery+BTAP, Tokyo,
Japan
"Re: Quest Japanese Contemporary Art since the 1970's"
Museum of Art, Seoul National University, Seoul, South Korea
"Parallel Views: Italian and Japanese Art from the 1950s, 60s
and 70s" The Warehouse, Dallas, USA

2012
"Tokyo 1955–1970: A New Avant-Garde" Museum of Modern
Art, New York, USA
"The 70s in Japan: 1968–1982" The Museum of Modern Art,
Saitama, Saitama, Japan
[traveled to Hiroshima City Museum of Contemporary Art,
Hiroshima, Japan]
"Paper Space: Drawings by Sculptors" Inman Gallery, Huston, USA
"Double Vision: Contemporary Art from Japan" Moscow
Museum of Modern Art, Moscow, Russia
[traveled to Tikotin Museum of Japanese Art / Haifa Museum of
Art, Haifa, Israel]
"Requiem for the Sun: The Art of Mono-ha" Blum & Poe, Los
Angeles, USA
[traveled to Gladstone Gallery, New York, USA]

2011
"Villa Tokyo" Various Locations in Kyobashi, Tokyo, Japan

2010
"Currents in Japanese Contemporary Wood Sculpture"
Hokkaido Museum of Modern Art, Sapporo, Hokkaido, Japan
"MOT Collection: Enter here -what do you see?" Museum of
Contemporary Art Tokyo, Tokyo, Japan
"Contemporary Art of China and Japan" Busan Museum of
Modern Art, Busan, South Korea

2009
"No Man's Land" Embassy of France in Tokyo, Tokyo, Japan

2008
"Mediations Biennale" The National Museum in Poznan, Poland
"Frieze Art Fair" Sculpture Park, London, UK
"Art Basel 39 Art Unlimited" Messe Basel, Basel, Switzerland

2007
"What is Mono-ha?" Tokyo Gallery+BTAP, Beijing, China
"Living in the Material World: 'things' in Art of the 20th Century
and Beyond" The National Art Center, Tokyo, Tokyo, Japan

2006
"Homage to Yoshiaki Tono" Gallery TOM, Tokyo, Japan
"Art and Object: Affinity of the Jomon and the Contemporary"
Aomori Museum of Art, Aomori, Japan
"Echigo-Tsumari Art Triennial 2006" Fukutake House,
Tokamachi, Niigata, Japan

2005
"Reconsidering Mono-ha" The National Museum of Art, Osaka,
Osaka, Japan

2004
"Remaking Modernism in Japan 1900–2000" Museum of
Contemporary Art Tokyo, Tokyo, Japan

2002
"Collaboration II: Kishio Suga & Mariko Hayashi" Gallery
Saiensu II, Morioka, Iwate, Japan
"The Unfinished Century: Legacies of 20th Century Art" The
National Museum of Modern Art, Tokyo, Tokyo, Japan

2001
"Collaboration: Kishio Suga & Mariko Hayashi" Gallery Saiensu
II, Morioka, Iwate, Japan
"Mono-ha: School of Things" Kettle's Yard, University of
Cambridge, Cambridge, UK
[traveled to Newlyn Art Gallery, Newlyn, UK]
"Global Visions: Art after 1980" Museum of Contemporary Art
Tokyo, Tokyo, Japan

2000
"The 3rd Gwangju Biennale" Biennale Hall, Jungoei Park, Gwangju,
South Korea

1999
"Mono-ha, Kishio Suga / Lee Ufan" M Gallery, Ashikaga, Tochigi,
Japan

1998
"Art / Ecosystem: The Contemporary Japanese Art Scene"
Utsunomiya Museum of Art, Utsunomiya, Tochigi, Japan

1997
"Gravity: Axis of Contemporary Art" The National Museum of
Art, Osaka, Osaka, Japan
"Beyond the Form" Chiba City Museum of Art, Chiba, Japan

1996
"Inside of Works, Outside of Works" Itabashi Art Museum, Tokyo,
Japan
"Prints of 1970's" The Shoto Museum of Modern Art, Tokyo, Japan
"Collection in Focus: 12 Installation Pieces" Museum of
Contemporary Art Tokyo, Tokyo, Japan

1995
"Kishio Suga + Mika Yoshizawa" Soh Gallery, Tokyo, Japan
"ASIANA Contemporary Art from The Far East" Palazzo
Vendramin Calergi, Venice, Italy
"Japanese Culture: The Fifty Postwar Years" Meguro Museum
of Art, Tokyo, Tokyo, Japan
[traveled to Hiroshima City Museum of Contemporary Art,
Hiroshima; Hyogo Prefectual Museum of Art, Kobe, Hyogo;
Fukuoka Prefectual Museum of Art, Fukuoka, Japan]

"Matter and Perception 1970: Mono-ha and the Search for
Fundamentals" Museum of Fine Arts, Gifu, Gifu, Japan
[traveled to Hiroshima City Museum of Contemporary Art,
Hiroshima; Kitakyushu Municipal Museum of Art, Kitakyushu,
Fukuoka; The Museum of Modern Art, Saitama, Saitama, Japan;
The Museum of Modern Art, St. Etienne, St. Etienne, France]

1994
"Mono-ha 1994 PART III" Kamakura Gallery, Tokyo, Japan
"The Domain of the Medium: New Approaches to the Medium
in Art, Craft, Design" Crafts Gallery, The National Museum of
Modern Art, Tokyo, Tokyo, Japan
"The 8th Triennale India" Lalit Kala Academy, New Delhi, India
"Japanese Art after 1945: Scream against the Sky" Yokohama
Museum of Art, Yokohama, Kanagawa, Japan
[traveled to Guggenheim Museum SoHo, New York; San
Francisco Museum of Modern Art; Yerba Buena Center for the
Arts, San Francisco, USA]
"Cross and Square: Grids" The Museum of Modern Art, Saitama,
Saitama, Japan

1992
"Avanguardie Giapponesi degli anni 70" Galleria Comunale
d'Arte Moderna di Bologna, Bologna, Italy
[traveled to The Setagaya Art Museum, Tokyo, Japan]

1991
"Movement of Contemporary Art in Japan: Three-Dimensional
Works, A Current of Contemporary Art in Japan" The Museum
of Modern Art, Toyama, Toyama, Japan
"70s–80s Contemporary Art: Mono-ha" Kamakura Gallery,
Tokyo, Japan
"The World of Box: do it yourself" Contemporary Art Gallery,
Mito, Mito, Ibaraki, Japan

1989
"The 20th Biennale Middleheim: Japan" Middelheim Open-Air
Museum for Sculpture, Antwerp, Belgium
"Art Exciting '89: beyond the today's being" The Museum of
Modern Art, Saitama, Saitama, Japan
["Japanese Ways, Western Means" traveled to Queensland
Museum, Brisbane, Australia]
"Wounded Surfaces: Lee Ufan, Kishio Suga, Koichi Ebitsuka,
Mika Yoshizawa" Soh Gallery, Tokyo, Japan
"The Space: Material, Tension, Vacancy in Japanese
Contemporary Art" The Museum of Modern Art, Saitama, Saitama,
Japan

1988
"Contemporary Art 1988 by Eleven Artists" Kahitsukan, Kyoto
Museum of Contemporary Art, Kyoto, Japan
"A Three weeks of symposium of color, shape and sound" Soh
Gallery, Tokyo, Japan
"Monoha: La scuola delle cose" Laboratorio di Arte
Contemporanea dell'Universita degli Studi di Roma "La Sapienza,"
Rome, Italy
"Introduction to Art History" Meguro Museum of Art, Tokyo,
Japan

1987
"The 2nd Biennale Japan Ushimado International Art Festival"
Ushimado Olive Garden, Setouchi, Okayama, Japan
"State of Contemporary Art from North Eastern Japan 2"

Fukushima Prefectural Museum of Art, Fukushima, Japan
"TAMA VIVANT '87: From Thingness to Narrative" Seed Hall,
Tokyo, Japan
"Art in Japan since 1969: Mono-ha and Post-Mono-ha" Seibu
Museum of Art, Tokyo, Japan

1986
"Japon des Avant-Gardes: 1910–1970" Centre Georges
Pompidou, Paris, France
"The 22nd Artists to-day '86: Apocalypse in Contemporary Art I:
from the depth of soul" Yokohama Civic Art Gallery, Yokohama,
Kanagawa, Japan
"Lee Ufan, Nobuo Sekine, Kishio Suga: Methods of the 1970s"
Soh Gallery, Tokyo, Japan
"Black and White in Art Today" The Museum of Modern Art,
Saitama, Saitama, Japan
"Mono-ha Part II" Kamakura Gallery, Tokyo, Japan
"Seoul Contemporary Asian Art Show" National Museum of
Modern Art, Seoul, South Korea
"monologue / dialogue Kishio Suga & Kenji Inumaki" Nabis
Gallery, Tokyo, Japan
"Contemporary Japanese Art" Taipei Fine Arts Museum, Taipei,
Taiwan
"The 2nd Tokyo Open-Air Contemporary Sculpture Exhibition
1986" Kinuta Park, Tokyo, Japan
"Seeing New Developments in Space and Materials" Institut
Franco-Japonaise de Tokyo, Tokyo, Japan

1985
"Opening Exhibition" Soh Gallery, Tokyo, Japan
"The 21st Artists Today '85: When Installations Become"
Yokohama Civic Art Gallery, Yokohama, Kanagawa, Japan
"The 2nd Asian Art Show" Fukuoka Art Museum, Fukuoka,
Japan
"Beauty of Wood: Between Painting and Sculpture" Hokkaido
Asahikawa Museum of Art, Asahikawa, Hokkaido, Japan
"40 Years of Japanese Contemporary Art Tokyo" Tokyo
Metropolitan Art Museum, Tokyo, Japan
"Construction in Japanese Paper" Halle Sud, Geneva,
Switzerland
"Artists' Books" Franklin Furnace Gallery, New York, USA
"Contemporary Sculpture in Japan: Wood" Kanagawa
Prefectural Gallery, Yokohama, Kanagawa, Japan

1984
"Trends of Contemporary Japanese Art 1970–1984: Universality
/ Individuality" Tokyo Metropolitan Art Museum, Tokyo, Japan
"State of Contemporary Art from North Eastern Japan"
Fukushima Prefectural Museum of Art, Fukushima, Japan
"The 2nd Toyama Now '84" Museum of Modern Art, Toyama,
Toyama, Japan
"Human Documents '84 / '85" Tokyo Gallery, Tokyo, Japan
"Japanese Contemporary Paintings 1960–1980" Gunma
Prefectural Museum of Modern Art, Takasaki, Gunma, Japan
"Sculpture in Modern Japan, 1968–1980s" Yamaguchi
Prefectural Museum of Art, Yamaguchi, Japan

1983
"A Panorama of Contemporary Art in Japanese Sculpture" The
Museum of Modern Art, Toyama, Toyama, Japan
"The Front of Contemporary Japanese Art" Isetan Museum of
Art, Tokyo, Japan
"A Sense of Contemporary Japanese Art 2: An Encounter with

the Sights around Us" The Miyagi Museum of Art, Sendai,
Miyagi, Japan
"Permanent Collection 2: Art of Today: Japan-England" Tokyo
Metropolitan Art Museum, Tokyo, Japan
"Shape and Spirit in Wood Works" The Museum of Modern Art,
Saitama, Saitama, Japan

1982
"Tama Art University Art Festival Exhibition" Tama Art
University Gallery, Tokyo, Japan
"Carnegie International" Carnegie Museum of Art, Pittsburgh,
USA
"The 4th Biennale of Sydney, Video / Performance Section" Art
Gallery of New South Wales, Sydney, Australia
"Arteder '82" Bilbao Art Center, Bilbao, Spain

1981
"Contemporary Art Exhibition of Japan: Trends of Japanese Art
in the 1970's" Korean Culture and Arts Foundation, Art Center,
Seoul, South Korea
"A Sense of Contemporary Japanese Art 1: An Encounter with
the Sights around Us" The Miyagi Museum of Art, Sendai,
Miyagi, Japan
"The 16th Sao Paulo Biennale" Parque Ibirapuera, Sao Paulo,
Brazil
"Kishio Suga, Susumu Koshimizu" Muramatsu Gallery, Tokyo,
Japan
"Performance in Video" Fukuoka Art Museum, Fukuoka, Japan
"The 1st Parallel Art Exhibition" Ohara Center of Tokyo, Tokyo,
Japan
"Yoin: Ideas from Japan made in Australia" Gryphon Gallery,
Victorian Collage of the Art, Melbourne, Australia

1980
"Variations on Planar Paintings" Fukuoka Art Museum,
Fukuoka, Japan
"1980 Japanese Prints" Tochigi Prefectural Museum,
Utsunomiya, Tochigi, Japan
"Shell Art Exhibition" Tokyo Central Museum, Tokyo, Japan

1979
"15th Artists Today" Yokohama Civic Art Gallery, Yokohama,
Kanagawa, Japan
"Lisbon International Show '79" Galeria de Belem-Lisbon,
Centro de Arte Contemporânea (Museu Nacional Soares dos
Reis), Lisbon, Portugal
"Kishio Suga, Masayuki Takahashi, Lee Ufan" Komai Gallery,
Tokyo, Japan

1978
"The 14th Artists Today" Yokohama Civic Art Gallery,
Yokohama, Kanagawa, Japan
"The 38th Venice Biennale" Japan Pavilion, Venice, Italy

1977
"The 13th Artists Today: The Richness of Painting" Yokohama
Civic Art Gallery, Yokohama, Kanagawa, Japan
"Japan and America: Contemporary Art Exhibition" 80 Ranton
Street Gallery, San Francisco, USA
[traveled to Kanagawa Prefectural Gallery, Yokohama,
Kanagawa, Japan]
"03・23・03: Projects / Performances / Conferences" Institut
d'art Contemporain, Montreal, Canada

1976
"The 2nd Biennale of Sydney: Recent International Forms in Art" Art Gallery of New South Wales, Sydney, Australia
"Seven Italian Artists and Seven Japanese Artists: Procedures Based on New Consciousness" Instituto Italiano di Cultura, Tokyo, Japan
"Ima: Now Exhibition" Ewing Gallery, University of Melbourne, Melbourne, Australia
"Kyoto Biennale: Contemporary Art by Seven Art Critics" Kyoto Municipal Museum of Art, Kyoto, Japan
"Pan-Conceptuals" Maki Gallery, Tokyo, Japan

1975
"Tokyo Gallery '76" Tokyo Gallery, Tokyo, Japan
"Japanese Contemporary Sculpture" Cranbrook Academy of Art, Bloomfield Hills, USA

1974
"7th Contemporary Form: Image Expression '74" Art Core Hall, Kyoto, Japan
"Materials" Van Abbe Museum, Eindhoven, the Netherlands
"Japan Art Exhibition" Louisiana Museum of Modern Art, Humlebaek, Denmark
 [traveled to Göteborgs Konstmuseum, Goteborg, Sweden; Henie Onstad Art Centre, Oslo, Norway]
"Universe (Cosmos): Image Experiments in Serigraphy by Contemporary Japanese Artists" Sao Paulo Museum of Art, Sao Paulo, Brazil
"Japan: Tradition und Gegenwart" Städtische Kunsthalle, Dusseldorf, Germany
"Katsurō Yoshida + Kishio Suga, Prints" Kaneko Art Gallery, Tokyo, Japan

1973
"8e Biennale de Paris" Musée d'Art Moderne de la Ville de Paris / Musée National d'Art Moderne, Paris, France
"The 8th Japan Art Festival" Tokyo Central Museum, Tokyo, Japan
[traveled to National Museum of Slovenia, Ljubljana, Slovenia; Städtische Kunsthalle, Dusseldorf, Germany]

1972
"The 1st Contemporary Japanese Graphics Exhibition" Institute of Contemporary Art, London, UK
"Project for Mount Vesuvius Operation" Minami Gallery, Tokyo, Japan
"International Art Exhibition" Il Centro Gallery, Naples, Italy

1971
"Print 1972" Shirota Gallery, Tokyo, Japan
"The 4th Contemporary Japanese Sculpture Exhibition" Ube Open-Air Museum, Ube, Yamaguchi, Japan
"The 10th Contemporary Art Exhibition of Japan" Tokyo Metropolitan Art Museum, Tokyo, Japan

1970
"The 5th Japan Art Festival Exhibition" The National Museum of Modern Art, Tokyo, Tokyo, Japan
["Contemporary Japanese Art" traveled to the Solomon R. Guggenheim Museum, New York, USA]
"The 7th Artists Today" Yokohama Civic Art Gallery, Yokohama, Kanagawa, Japan
"August 1970: Aspects of New Japanese Art" The National

Museum of Modern Art, Tokyo, Tokyo, Japan
"The 9th Trends in Contemporary Art" The National Museum of Modern Art, Kyoto, Kyoto, Japan

1968
"The 9 Visional Points" Muramatsu Gallery, Tokyo, Japan
"00X Exhibition: Tama Fine Art College 00X Class" Muramatsu Gallery, Tokyo, Japan

1967
"OOOPLAN" Muramatsu Gallery, Tokyo, Japan
"Universiade Exhibition" Isetan Department Store, Tokyo, Japan
"The 11th Shell Art Award" Shirokiya, Tokyo, Japan
[traveled to Kyoto Municipal Museum of Art, Kyoto, Japan]
"N・S・S" Tsubaki Kindai Gallery, Tokyo, Japan
"OOOPLAN 8 Events for Midnight" Shinjuku Pit Inn, Tokyo, Japan
"The 4th International Young Artists Exhibition" Seibu Department Store, Tokyo, Japan

Selected Activations (Performance)

All "Events" were renamed "Activations" in March 2004

2017
"Determined Presence, Predisposed Absence" Yokohama Museum of Art, Yokohama, Kanagawa, Japan

2016
"Separating Spaces" Yokohama Civic Art Gallery, Yokohama, Kanagawa, Japan
"Centered Condition, Circulated Space" Pirelli HangarBicocca, Milan, Italy

2015
"Multiple Latent Sceneries" Museum of Contemporary Art Tokyo, Tokyo, Japan

2014
"Scattering and Gathering" Vangi Sculpture Garden Museum, Nagaizumi, Shizuoka, Japan

2009
"Cultivated Path of Wind" Itamuro Onsen Daikokuya, Nasushiobara, Tochigi, Japan

2008
"Edges of Space" Itamuro Onsen Daikokuya, Nasushiobara, Tochigi, Japan
"Appearance of Multiple Latencies" Messe Basel, Basel, Switzerland

2006
"System of Plurality" Fukutake House, Tokamachi, Niigata, Japan
"Appearance of Multiple Conflicted Causes" Itamuro Onsen Daikokuya, Nasushiobara, Tochigi, Japan
"Concurrent Correspondence" Tomio Koyama Gallery, Tokyo, Japan

2005
"Divided Rhythm" Iwate Museum of Art, Morioka, Iwate, Japan

2004
"Edge of Space" Yokohama Museum of Art, Yokohama, Kanagawa, Japan

1998
"Points of Complexity" Chiba City Museum of Art, Chiba, Japan
"Towards Stability and Instability" Kanagawa Prefectural Gallery, Yokohama, Kanagawa, Japan
"Unfolding Field" Yamaguchi Prefectural Art Museum, Yamaguchi, Japan
"Stability of Separation and Conjunction: Visual Interstices" Itami City Museum of Art, Itami, Hyogo, Japan

1997
"Gathered Release—Restriction" Hiroshima City Museum of Contemporary Art, Hiroshima, Japan

1995
Kitakyushu Municipal Museum of Art, Kitakyushu, Fukuoka, Japan
"Distribution of Polysemy" Hiroshima City Museum of Contemporary Art, Hiroshima, Japan

1990
"Along Intervals" Touko Museum of Contemporary Art, Tokyo, Japan
"Surrounding Construction–910" Concept Space R2, Takasaki, Gunma, Japan

1987
"EXTEND: 50th Anniversary of Tama Art University: TAMABIVENTS" Studio 200, Tokyo, Japan

1986
"Exposed Way to the Sky" Yokohama Civic Art Gallery, Yokohama, Kanagawa, Japan

1984
"Edges in Motion" The Museum of Modern Art, Toyama, Toyama, Japan

1981
Fukuoka Art Museum, Fukuoka, Japan
"Place Continuity" Inokashira Park, Tokyo, Japan
"SHEbbING" PARCO, Tokyo, Japan

1980
"Entirety of Transferred Units" Gallery Lumiere, Yamagata, Japan
"Progression of Space" Kaneko Art Gallery, Tokyo, Japan
"Matter and Location" Gallery Saiensu, Morioka, Iwate, Japan
"Matter and Dimension" Kaneko Art Gallery, Tokyo, Japan

1979
Yokohama Civic Art Gallery, Yokohama, Kanagawa, Japan

1978
"Adaptation-Circumstances-Transition-Substance" Tama Art University, Hachioji Campus, Tokyo, Japan
Japan Pavilion, Venice, Italy

1977
Inokashira Park, Tokyo, Japan
"Theory of Emerging Situation" Tokiwa Park, Tokyo, Japan
"Theory for Creating Sites" Maki Gallery, Tokyo, Japan

1976
"Differentiated Movement: Continuous Existence" Instituto Italiano di Cultura, Tokyo, Japan
"Dependent Law" International Christian University, Tokyo, Japan
"There: at Each Location" Maki Gallery, Tokyo, Japan
"For the Side Corners" Kyoto Municipal Museum of Art, Kyoto, Japan
"Phase Getting Fulfilled" Maki Gallery, Tokyo, Japan

1975
"Phase of Acquisition" Maki Gallery, Tokyo, Japan
"Gathered Space" Maki Gallery, Tokyo, Japan
"Natural Order" Tokiwa Park, Tokyo, Japan

1974
"Units of Dependency" Tamura Gallery, Tokyo, Japan
"Fieldology" galerie 16, Kyoto, Japan

1973
"Law of Dependence" Tamura Gallery, Tokyo, Japan
"Parallel Perception: Independent Existence" Artist's studio, Tokyo, Japan

Selected Fieldwork

1977
"Order of Sky" Inokashira Park, Tokyo, Japan

1974
"Floating Units of Existence, Law of Immutability, Surrounding Units, Space-Order, Spatial Units, Elements of Dependency, Components of Space, Units of Spatial Dependency, Spatial Existence, Surrounding Dependency" Yomiuri Land / Tama River, Kawasaki, Kanagawa, Japan

1973
"In the State of Equal Dimension" Inokashira Park, Tokyo, Japan
"Spatial Body" Inokashira Park, Tokyo, Japan

1972
"Unfolding Field" Rooftop of Joshuya Building, Tokyo, Japan
"Situated Condition" Artist's studio, Tokyo, Japan

1971
"Situation in Space" Inokashira Park, Tokyo, Japan

1969
"Rise of Vanishing Point" Wakabayashi, Tokyo, Japan
"Diagonal Phase" Fujimicho Studio, Yokohama, Kanagawa, Japan
"Surface Phase" Wakabayashi, Tokyo, Japan

1968
"Layered Space" Artist's studio, Kanagawa, Japan

Activation *Multiple Latent Sceneries*
March 7, 2015 at Museum of Contemporary Art Tokyo ("Kishio Suga: Situated Latency")
68 mins. Digital data
Filmed by Tsuyoshi Satoh, Tomio Koyama Gallery
Courtesy of Tsuyoshi Satoh
Photo by Tsuyoshi Satoh

Event *Progression of Space*
September 29, 1980 at Kaneko Art Gallery ("Flattened Phase: In Terms of Phenomena")
41 mins. Digital data
Filmed by Video Information Center
©VIC | courtesy of Keio University Art Center
Photo by Tasaku Kaneko

Activation *Divided Rhythm*
September 3, 2005 at Iwate Museum of Art ("Uncertain Void: Installation by Kishio Suga")
71 mins. Digital data
Filmed by Iwate Museum of Art
Photo by Tsuyoshi Satoh

Event *Adaptation-Circumstances-Transition-Substance*
November 2, 1978 at Tama Art University, Hachioji Campus
39 mins. Digital data
Filmed by Yasuhiko Suga
Courtesy of Tomio Koyama Gallery
Photo by Shigeo Anzaï © Estate of Shigeo Anzaï, courtesy of Zeit-Foto

Event *Surrounding Construction–910*
January 28, 1990 at Concept Space R2
41 mins. Digital data
Filmed by Tsuyoshi Satoh   Courtesy of Tomio Koyama Gallery
Photo by Tsuyoshi Satoh

パブリック・コレクション　Public Collections

秋田県立近代美術館、秋田	Akita Museum of Modern Art, Yokote, Akita, Japan
いわき市立美術館、福島	Busan Museum of Art, Busan, South Korea
岩手県立美術館、岩手	Chiba City Museum of Art, Chiba, Japan
ヴァンジ彫刻庭園美術館、静岡	Daegu Art Museum, Daegu, South Korea
宇都宮美術館、栃木	Dallas Museum of Art, Dallas, USA
鴨緑江美術館、丹青、中国	Dia Art Foundation, New York, USA
何必館 京都現代美術館、京都	Fuchu City, Hiroshima, Japan
北九州市立美術館、福岡	Glenstone Foundation, Potomac, USA
グッゲンハイム・アブダビ、アブダビ、アラブ首長国連邦	Guggenheim Abu Dhabi, Abu Dhabi, UAE
グレンストーン財団、ポトマック、アメリカ	Hara Museum ARC, Shibukawa, Gunma, Japan
国立近代美術館（ポンピドゥ・センター）、パリ、フランス	He Art Museum, Foshan, China
国立国際美術館、大阪	Hiroshima City Museum of Contemporary Art, Hiroshima, Japan
埼玉県立近代美術館、埼玉	Hirshhorn Museum and Sculpture Garden, Washington, DC, USA
菅木志雄倉庫美術館、栃木	Hokkaido Asahikawa Museum of Art, Asahikawa, Hokkaido, Japan
スコットランド国立近代美術館、エジンバラ、イギリス	Iwaki City Art Musum, Iwaki, Fukushima, Japan
スマート美術館（シカゴ大学）、シカゴ、アメリカ	Iwate Museum of Art, Morioka, Iwate, Japan
高橋龍太郎コレクション、東京	Kahitsukan, Kyoto Museum of Contemporary Art, Kyoto, Japan
高松市美術館、香川	Kishio Suga Souko Museum, Nasushiobara, Tochigi, Japan
ダラス美術館、ダラス、アメリカ	Kitakyushu Municipal Museum of Art, Kitakyushu, Fukuoka, Japan
千葉市美術館、千葉	The Laboratory of Contemporary Art at Sapienza University of Rome, Rome, Italy
ディア美術財団、ニューヨーク、アメリカ	Long Museum, Shanghai, China
大邱美術館、大邱、韓国	M+, Hong Kong
テート・モダン、ロンドン、イギリス	Margulies Collection at the Warehouse, Miami, USA
東京国立近代美術館、東京	Meguro Museum of Art, Tokyo, Tokyo, Japan
東京都現代美術館、東京	The Miyagi Museum of Art, Sendai, Miyagi, Japan
富山県美術館、富山	Museum of Contemporary Art Tokyo, Tokyo, Japan
ニューヨーク近代美術館、ニューヨーク、アメリカ	The Museum of Modern Art, New York, USA
ハーシュホーン美術館彫刻庭園、ワシントンD.C.、アメリカ	The Museum of Modern Art, Saitama, Saitama, Japan
原美術館ARC、群馬	The Museum of Modern Art, Toyama, Toyama, Japan
ピノー・コレクション	Museum Voorlinden, Wassenaar, the Netherlands
広島市現代美術館、広島	The National Museum of Art, Osaka, Osaka, Japan
フォーリンデン美術館、ワッセナー、オランダ	The National Museum of Modern Art (The Centre Pompidou), Paris, France
釜山市立美術館、釜山、韓国	The National Museum of Modern Art, Tokyo, Tokyo, Japan
府中市、広島	Pinault Collection
北海道立旭川美術館、北海道	The Rachofsky Collection, Dallas, USA
マルグリーズ・コレクション、マイアミ、アメリカ	Rakusui-tei Museum of Art, Toyama, Japan
宮城県美術館、宮城	Scottish National Gallery of Modern Art, Edinburgh, UK
目黒区美術館、東京	Smart Museum of Art, The University of Chicago, Chicago, USA
山口県立美術館、山口	Takahashi Ryutaro Collection, Tokyo, Japan
横浜市民ギャラリー、神奈川	Takamatsu Art Museum, Takamatsu, Kagawa, Japan
横浜美術館、神奈川	Tate Modern, London, UK
楽翠亭美術館、富山	UBS Art Collection
ラチョフスキー・コレクション、ダラス、アメリカ	Utsunomiya Museum of Art, Utsunomiya, Tochigi, Japan
ローマ大学付属現代美術実験美術館、ローマ、イタリア	Vangi Sculpture Garden Museum, Nagaizumi, Shizuoka, Japan
龍美術館、上海、中国	Yalu River Art Museum, Dandong, China
和美術館、仏山、中国	Yamaguchi Prefectural Art Museum, Yamaguchi, Japan
M+、香港	Yokohama Civic Art Gallery, Yokohama, Kanagawa, Japan
UBS アートコレクション	Yokohama Museum of Art, Yokohama, Kanagawa, Japan

主要参考文献（2015年−） | Selected Bibliography (2015−)

凡例：
・作家、小山登美夫ギャラリー、佐藤毅氏より提供された資料に基づき、2015年以降に刊行された文献を編集した。
・菅木志雄の「自著」「自筆文献」および「個展カタログ」「グループ展カタログ」「関連書籍」「逐次刊行物」の項目から成る。
・項目ごとに、刊行年月日の降順に示した。
・ウェブサイトの最終アクセス日はすべて2021年11月9日。
・2014年以前の文献については『菅木志雄 置かれた潜在性』（東京都現代美術館編、HeHe、2015年）を参照されたい。

Notes:
・ This bibliography, comprised of materials published in and after 2015, is based on materials provided by the artist, Tomio Koyama Gallery and
  Tsuyoshi Satoh.
・ This bibliography is divided into six sections: books by Kishio Suga, writings by Kishio Suga, solo exhibition catalogues, group exhibition
  catalogues, related books and periodicals.
・ The items in each category are arranged in descending chronological order.
・ All websites were last accessed on November 9, 2021.
・ For a bibliography prior to 2015, refer to *Kishio Suga: Situated Latency* (ed. Museum of Contemporary Art Tokyo, HeHe, 2015).

自著 | Books by Kishio Suga

- *Kishio Suga Writings, Vol. I: 1969–1979*, Milan: Skira editore / Los Angeles: Blum & Poe / Sao Paulo: Mendes Wood DM, 2021
- 『世界を〈放置〉する ものと場の思想集成』ぷねうま舎、2016年
- 『双天のゴライアス』ヴァンジ彫刻庭園美術館、2015年

自筆文献 | Writings by Kishio Suga

- 菅木志雄「放たれた空因」『ユリイカ』12月臨時増刊号 No. 751、青土社、2019年11月、pp. 107–112
- 菅木志雄「交遊抄 ふわりとして」『日経新聞』2016年6月11日、40面
- Kishio Suga, trans. Ashley Rawlings, "Reflections: Kishio Suga," *ArtAsiaPacific Almanac 2016*, Hong Kong: ArtAsiaPacific
  Publishing LLC., 2016, pp. 204–205 [http://www.artasiapacific.com/Magazine/Almanac2016/KishioSuga]

個展カタログ | Solo Exhibition Catalogues

- 『菅木志雄 集められた〈中間〉』小山登美夫ギャラリー、2021年
  菅木志雄「集められた〈中間〉」p. 5；天野太郎「集められた〈中間〉—あるいは〈中間〉の多義性」pp. 74–79
  Kishio Suga: Gathered <Intermediates>, Tokyo: Tomio Koyama Gallery, 2021
  Kishio Suga, "Gathered <Intermediates>," p. 7; Taro Amano, "Gathered intermediates: or, the ambiguity of the intermediate," pp. 80–87
- 『菅木志雄 初期作品集』ギャラリー古今、2020年
  佐藤春喜「始まり」p. 7；「菅語録」p. 79；菅木志雄「在るべくしてものはあった」p. 80
  Kishio Suga: Early Works from the Haruki Collection, Tokyo: Gallery Cocon, 2020
  Haruki Sato, "The Beginning," p. 7; Statements by Kishio Suga, p. 79; Kishio Suga, "Things Existed as They Should," p. 81
- 『菅木志雄 放たれた景空』小山登美夫ギャラリー、2020年
  菅木志雄「放たれた景空」p. 5；吉竹美香「空隙（ヴォイド）を解放する」pp. 74–79
  Kishio Suga: Released Scenic Space, Tokyo: Tomio Koyama Gallery, 2020
  Kishio Suga, "Released Scenic Space," p. 7; Mika Yoshitake, "Freeing the Void," pp. 80–86
- 『菅木志雄 測られた区体』小山登美夫ギャラリー、2019年
  菅木志雄「測られた区体」p. 5；長谷川祐子「ほとんどすべて—菅木志雄のメイキング」pp. 82–87
  Kishio Suga: Measured Divisional Entities, Tokyo: Tomio Koyama Gallery, 2019
  Kishio Suga, "Measured Divisional Entities," p. 7; Yuko Hasegawa, "Almost Everything: The Making of Kishio Suga," pp. 88–96
- 『菅木志雄 広げられた自空 / 分けられた指空性』小山登美夫ギャラリー、2018年
  菅木志雄「現れるもの、現れないもの」p. 4；片岡真実「『状況』に探りをいれる」pp. 34–39；菅木志雄「有と無のあいだで」p. 52
  Kishio Suga: Expanded Self Space / Divided Orientation of Space, Tokyo: Tomio Koyama Gallery, 2018

Kishio Suga, "What Emerges, and Does Not Emerge," p. 6; Mami Kataoka, "Probing 'situations'," pp. 40–49; Kishio Suga, "Between Existence of Non-Existence," p. 54

- 『菅木志雄 志向する界景』小山登美夫ギャラリー、2017年
  菅木志雄「志向する界景」p. 4；松井みどり「ものの眺め、人の地点：菅木志雄の芸術実践における心とものの相互依存」pp. 82–90
  Kishio Suga: Intentional Scenic Space, Tokyo: Tomio Koyama Gallery, 2017
  Kishio Suga, "Intentional Scenic Space," p. 6; Midori Matsui, "The Presence of Things, the Position of People: The Interdependance of Mind and Matter in Kishio Suga's Artistic Practice," pp. 92–103
- Yuko Hasegawa and Vicente Todolí (eds.), *Kishio Suga: Situations*, Milan: Mousse Publishing / Milan: Pirelli HangarBicocca, 2016
  Yuko Hasegawa, "For Inaction: Thoughts on Kishio Suga," pp. 13–30 / "Per inazione: Riflessioni su Kishio Suga," pp. 31–47; Achille Bonito Oliva, "Ars Brevis at the School of Things," pp. 49–51 / "Arte breve a scuola delle cose," pp. 53–56; Barbara Bertozzi, "The Language of Things: Theory and Artistic Production of Mono-ha," pp. 57–72 / "Il linguaggio delle cose: Teoria e produzione artistica del gruppo Mono-ha," pp. 73–86; Kishio Suga, [Essays], pp. 87–112 / [Scritti], pp. 87–112
- 『菅木志雄』ヴァンジ彫刻庭園美術館、2015年
  菅木志雄「集存の開空」pp. 6–11；千葉成夫「菅木志雄論—地に身、間に惑、空に考」pp. 14–25；吉竹美香「菅木志雄の制作の基本とアクティヴェイションの構造」pp. 26–37；森啓輔「菅木志雄—境界線上の身体」pp. 38–48；佐藤毅「集写助友」pp. 50–51；菅木志雄「転移空間」pp. 82–87；森啓輔「『転移空間』解題」pp. 90–97；菅木志雄「みえない世界のみえない言語」pp. 98–101；菅木志雄「〈放置〉という状況」pp. 102–106；菅木志雄「場の論理—アースワークによせて」pp. 107–114；菅木志雄「周辺を束ねて界端を開く」pp. 115–122；峯村敏明「菅木志雄論のために（思想篇）」pp. 126–134；建畠晢「ヒエラルキーなき空間」pp. 135–137；谷新「もうひとつの菅木志雄論」pp. 138–145；倉石信乃「事実のエチカ—菅木志雄ノート」pp. 146–160；森啓輔「菅木志雄を読み解くキーワード」pp. 162–163
  Kishio Suga, Shizuoka: Vangi Sculpture Garden Museum, 2015
  Kishio Suga, "The Open Space of Gathered Existing," pp. 229–224; Shigeo Chiba, "On Kishio Suga: Body to the Earth, Feelings to the Space Between, Thoughts to the Sky," pp. 223–212; Mika Yoshitake, "Suga's Fundamentals and the Structures of Activation," pp. 211–202; Keisuke Mori, "Kishio Suga: Body on the Boundary Line," pp. 201–190
- Museum of Contemporary Art Tokyo (ed.), *Kishio Suga: Situated Latency*, HeHe, 2015
  Kishio Suga, "Latent Infinity," pp. 75–79; Naoko Seki; "Traces of Thought: Kishio Suga's Production Notebooks," pp. 140–161; Yuko Hasegawa, "Thoughts on Kishio Suga," pp. 162–175; Simon Groom, "Framing Suga," pp. 176–181
  東京都現代美術館（編）『菅木志雄 置かれた潜在性』HeHe、2015年
  菅木志雄「潜在無限」pp. 80–83；関直子「思考の航跡—菅木志雄の制作ノート」pp. 140–161；長谷川祐子「菅木志雄論」pp. 182–188；サイモン・グルーム「菅作品をフレーミングする」pp. 189–191
- Karen Jacobson (ed.), *Kishio Suga*, New York: Blum&Poe, 2015
  Jason Farago, "The Disorder of Things," pp. 8–15

グループ展カタログ ｜ Group Exhibition Catalogues

- 『多摩美の版画、50年』多摩美術大学美術館、2021年
- 国立新美術館、國華社、朝日新聞社（編）『古典×現代2020 時空を超える日本のアート』朝日新聞社、2020年
  長屋光枝「時を超えた対話—古典と現代」pp. 11–17；「1章　仙厓×菅木志雄」pp. 20–33
  National Art Center, Tokyo, Kokkasha, The Asahi Shimbun (eds.), *TIMELESS CONVERSATIONS 2020: Voices from Japanese Art of the Past and Present*, Tokyo: The Asahi Shimbun, 2020
  "Chapter 1 Sengai x SUGA Kishio," pp. 20–33; Mitsue Nagaya, "Timeless Conversations Between Past and Present," pp. 236–240
- 国立新美術館、國華社、朝日新聞社（編）『古典×現代2020 時空を超える日本のアート　展覧会ドキュメント』朝日新聞社、2020年
  「1章　仙厓×菅木志雄」pp. 5–12
  National Art Center, Tokyo, Kokkasha, The Asahi Shimbun (eds.), *TIMELESS CONVERSATIONS 2020: Voices from Japanese Art of the Past and Present: Documents*, Tokyo: The Asahi Shimbun, 2020
  "Chapter 1 Sengai x SUGA Kishio," pp. 5–12
- 『DECODE／出来事と記録—ポスト工業化社会の美術』埼玉県立近代美術館／多摩美術大学、2020年
- 소장품 100선, 大邱：大邱美術館、2020
- 『横浜美術館開館30周年記念 Meet the Collection —アートと人と、美術館』横浜美術館、2019年
  松永真太郎「モノからはじめる」pp. 86–87；菅木志雄「展覧会に寄せて」pp. 88–89
  30th Anniversary of the Yokohama Museum of Art: Meet the Collection, Yokohama: Yokohama Museum of Art, 2019
  Matsunaga Shintaro, "Beginning with a Material," pp. 86–87; Kishio Suga, "Statement by SUGA Kishio," pp. 88–89
- 東京都現代美術館（編）『百年の編み手たち 流動する日本の近現代美術』美術出版社、2019年
  Museum of Contemporary Art Tokyo (ed.), *Weavers of Worlds: A Century of Flux in Japanese Modern / Contemporary Art*, Tokyo: Bijutsu Shuppan-sha Co., Ltd., 2019
- 『横浜市民ギャラリーコレクション展2019 昭和後期の現代美術—1964～1989—』横浜市民ギャラリー、2019年
  p. 6；大塚真弓「創造の場所」pp. 3–4
- 『1968年—激動の時代の芸術』千葉市美術館他、2018年
  pp. 226, 228–229；川谷承子「もの派の台頭」pp. 220–221

- Russell Storer, Eugene Tan (eds.), *Minimalism: Space. Light. Object*, Singapore: National Gallery Singapore, 2018, p. 134
- Anna Katherine Brodbeck (ed.), *Two x Two x Twenty*, Dallas: Dallas Museum of Art, 2018, pp. 18, 192–193
- Catherine Wood, *Performance in Contemporary Art*, London: Tate Publishing, 2018, pp. 194–195
- 『安齊重男による日本の70年代美術』国立国際美術館、2017年
  Japanese Art of the 1970s through the Photography of Anzaï Shigeo, Osaka: The National Museum of Art, Osaka, 2017
- *Japanorama: Nouveau regard sur la création contemporaine*, Paris: Centre Pompidou-Metz, 2017, pp. 136–137, 208–209
- 『陶芸⇆現代美術の関係性ってどうなってんだろう？ 現代美術の系譜に陶芸の文脈も入れ込んで』Kaikai Kiki Gallery、2017年
  What Is the Relationship Between Ceramics and Contemporary Art? (Considering the Context of Ceramics in the Lineage of Contemporary Art), Tokyo: Kaikai Kiki Gallery, 2017
- *Viva Arte Viva: 57. Esposizione Internazionale d'Arte: La Biennale Di Venezia: MOSTRA*, Venice: La Biennale di Venezia, 2017, pp. 522–525
- *Karla Black and Kishio Suga: A New Order*, Edinburgh: National Galleries of Scotland, 2017
  John Leighton, Simon Groom, "Director's Foreword," p. 5; Kishio Suga, "Between 'Presence' and 'Nothingness'(2005)," pp. 7–8
- 『新・今日の作家展2016 創造の場所—もの派から現代へ』横浜市民ギャラリー、2016年
  p.7；大塚真弓（聞き手）「菅木志雄インタビュー」pp. 8–9
- 『高橋コレクション展 ミラー・ニューロン』玄光社、2015年
  pp. 20–21, 140；堀元彰「来るべき時代のカルテ—高橋コレクションについて」pp. 144–147
- *Mono-ha*, Milan: Fondazione Mudima, 2015
  pp. 330–348, 425–428; Yasuyuki Nakai, "Reconsidering Mono-ha," pp. 39–73; Kiyoshi Okada, "The Challenge to Contemporary Art: Materials and Mono-ha," pp. 119–133; Masahiro Aoki, "What Is 'Mono-ha' and Why 'Mono'?," pp. 157–173
  『Mono-ha』ムディマ財団、2015年
  中井康之「もの派—再考」pp.75–117；岡田潔「現代美術への問い 物質からの探究ともの派をめぐって」pp.135–153；青木正弘「"もの派"とは何であったか。また、なぜ"もの"なのか。」pp.177–199
  Mono-ha, Milano: Fondazione Mudima, 2015
  Yasuyuki Nakai, "Riesaminare Mono-ha," pp. 74–116; Kiyoshi Okada; "La sfida contemporanea: i materiali e Mono-ha," pp. 134–155; Masahiro Aoki, "Che cosa e 'Mono-ha', e perche 'mono'?," pp. 176–206

関連書籍 ｜ Related Books

- 『開廊70周年記念 東京画廊70年』東京画廊＋BTAP、2021年、p.29
- 千葉成夫『増補 現代美術逸脱史 1945〜1985』筑摩書房、2021年
  「第三章『もの派』」pp.173–241；「増補 この先へ Ⅰ『もの派』の展開と変容 菅木志雄—空間＝時間のたて・よこ」pp.344–350
- Penny Florence, *Thinking the Sculpture Garden: Art, Plant, Landscape*, London: Routledge, 2020, pp. 31–33, 60–69
- Jori Finkel, *It Speaks to Me: Art That Inspires Artists*, Munich: Prestel, 2019, pp. 92–93, 154
- 本阿弥清『"もの派"の起源—石子順造・李禹煥・グループ"幻触"がはたした役割』水声社、2016年

逐次刊行物 ｜ Periodicals

- 大西若人「東京・六本木で菅木志雄展」『朝日新聞』2020年9月8日（夕刊）、3面
- 井上晋治「古典の名品と現代作家 共演 東京・六本木国立新美術館」『読売新聞』2020年8月6日、27面
- 高木友絵「重なり、結びつく感性『古典×現代2020 時空を超える日本のアート』」『朝日新聞』2020年7月11日、16面
- "Collector Matthew Shieh: Five Selected Artworks," *Ocula*, May 7, 2020 [https://ocula.com/magazine/insights/collector-matthew-shieh-five-selected-artworks/]
- 千葉恵理子「蔵出し美術展：名作へ、多様なアプローチ『古典×現代2020』」『朝日新聞』2020年4月21日（夕刊）、3面
- アンドリュー・マークル「労働、流通、移民、そして復讐：ヤン・ヴォーを語るための言葉」『国立国際美術館ニュース』第237号、国立国際美術館、2020年4月、pp.2–3
- 濱淵真弓「土曜美術館：菅木志雄『囲間内奥』枠内に影と空間生み出す」『読売新聞』岩手版 2020年3月28日、24面
- 「スペシャルインタビュー2 菅木志雄さん」『Discover Japan』Vol.102、ディスカバー・ジャパン、2020年3月、p.37
- 「日本美術、新旧で対比『古典×現代2020』展 3月から東京・国立新美術館」『秋田魁新報』2020年1月8日、8面
- 「ものと空間の関係性 あすまで彩園子 菅さんインスタレーション」『盛岡タイムス』2019年10月11日、3面
- 「緊張感のある空間 盛岡出身・菅木志雄さん個展」『岩手日報』2019年10月7日、14面
- 楊椀茹「『反界結端』綜覧 菅木志雄的創作内核」『今藝術＆投資』、台北：典蔵、2019年10月、pp.142–145
- 「長い時間をかけて探り続ける『もの』。菅木志雄インタビュー」『美術手帖』（ウェブ版）、美術出版社、2019年7月10日 [https://bijutsutecho.com/magazine/magazine/interview/20095]
- 永田晶子「『もの派』中核・菅さん木枠用い多彩に表現 六本木で個展」『毎日新聞』2019年7月3日（夕刊）、4面
- 黒沢綾子「菅木志雄の個展 色合いの違いを探して」『産経新聞』2019年6月30日、10面

- 大西若人「名品を包む現役作家の視点　横浜美術館開館30周年記念展、4人が学芸員と協働」『朝日新聞』2019年5月14日（夕刊）、3面
- 「現代美術家が新たな光　横浜美術館開館30周年記念展　Meet the Collection　アートと人と、美術館」『神奈川新聞』2019年4月22日、12面
- 「平成28（2016）年美術界年史：1月：毎日芸術賞受賞者決定」『日本美術年鑑』平成29年版、東京文化財研究所、2019年3月、p.1
- Michael Do, "An unopened packet of biscuits: a studio visit with Kishio Suga," *Center for Contemporary Asian Art*, December 2018 [http://www.4a.com.au/4a_papers_article/kishio-suga-micheal-do/]
- 「"もの"で新たな状況　彩園子で13日まで　菅木志雄さん（盛岡出身）個展」『盛岡タイムス』2018年10月8日、3面
- 「身近な素材、空間に命　盛岡　菅木志雄さん古里個展」『岩手日報』2018年10月6日、19面
- 桐谷麗了子「麗了子がめぐる写真についてのニ、三の事柄57　写す行為、写っている状況　両者の関係そのものを宙吊りにする菅木志雄の作品」『日本カメラ』第932号、日本カメラ社、2018年9月、p.179
- 大西若人「木や石の存在　ズレ心地よく　菅木志雄展」『朝日新聞』2018年6月26日（夕刊）、4面
- 森田睦「菅木志雄さん個展、都内3会場同時に」『読売新聞』2018年6月14日、21面
- 永田晶子「アートピックス：『もの派』菅さん　三つの個展　思考と表現を体感」『毎日新聞』2018年6月13日（夕刊）、4面
- Dawn Chan, "Kishio Suga at Blum & Poe," *Artforum*, Vol.56, No. 9, New York: Artforum, May 2018, p. 232
- "Goings On About Town: Kishio Suga," *New Yorker*, New York: Condé Nast, April 16, 2018, p. 11
- Colin Edgington, "Kishio Suga," *Brooklyn Rail*, April 4, 2018 [https://brooklynrail.org/2018/04/artseen/KISHIO-SUGA]
- 「集客の要として注目されるアート」『TAMABI news』Vol. 76、多摩美術大学、2018年2月、p. 6
- 森田睦「生老病死の旅路：『もの』とは何か　深く考察　菅木志雄さん」『読売新聞』2018年1月27日（夕刊）、5面
- Giovanni Ferrario, "Ri. Relazioni estetiche tra Oriente ed Ofccidente a partire da Kishio Suga," *Studi di Estetica*, N. 10, 1/2018, Bologna: Mimesis, 2018, pp. 125–136
- 「那須塩原『アートな街』に　市が戦略策定へ　板室街道沿い施設活用」『読売新聞』栃木版　2017年12月19日、29面
- 田中えり「菅木志雄さん新作20点　空間に溶け込む造形美　那須塩原」『下野新聞』2017年11月25日、16面
- 吉井仁実「現代アート一歩近づく12stories　第10回　もの派」『25ans』No. 457、ハースト婦人画報社、2017年8月、p.18
- 「あのアートが見たい。」『Pen』No. 433、CCCメディアハウス、2017年8月、pp.24–28
- Kishio Suga, trans. Mika Yoshitake, "Interview: Kishio Suga," *Artforum.com*, July 24, 2017 [https://www.artforum.com/interviews/kishio-suga-discusses-his-show-at-dia-chelsea-69933]
- Brian Boucher, "The Dia Art Foundation Expands Its Focus to Asian Art, Making Key New Acquisitions," *Artnet News*, July 10, 2017 [https://news.artnet.com/art-world/dia-acquires-lee-ufan-kishio-suga-1015706]
- Carolyn Twersky, "Dia Art Foundation Acquires Works by Lee Ufan and Kishio Suga," *Artnews*, July 10, 2017 [https://www.artnews.com/art-news/news/dia-art-foundation-acquires-works-by-lee-ufan-and-kishio-suga-8667/]
- 「『シェル美術賞2017』菅木志雄氏インタビューを公開　～第11回シェル美術賞1等受賞作家～」『石油政策』第56巻第1475号、セントラル通信社、2017年6月25日、pp.10–12
- 「新たな表現の可能性　ベネチア国際美術展　ドイツ館金獅子賞　観客を主体的鑑賞にいざなう」『愛媛新聞』2017年6月11日、17面
- 黒沢綾子「『活性化』する空間　菅木志雄」『産経新聞』2017年6月1日、15面
- 「勅使河原茜　個展　HANA SO」『草月』No. 333、草月文化事業株式会社、2017年6月、pp.4–5、19
- 「受賞・入選者インタビュー Vol.7　菅木志雄」『出光興産』2017年6月 [https://www.idemitsu.com/jp/enjoy/culture_art/art/interview/vol7.html]
- 永田晶子「海外でも注目の美術家　菅木志雄さん新作個展　東京・六本木」『毎日新聞』2017年5月17日（夕刊）、6面
- 丸山ひかり「国家を自然を問い直す　ベネチア・ビエンナーレ」『朝日新聞』2017年5月30日（夕刊）、4面
- Seph Rodney, "The Persistence of Things in a Japanese Minimalist's Installations," *Hyperallergic*, May 26, 2017 [https://hyperallergic.com/380774/kishio-suga-dia-chelsea/]
- Jennifer S Li, "Kishio Suga at Blum & Poe," *Art in America*, New York: Brant Publications, May 2017, pp. 135–136
- Lindsay Preston Zappas, "Would You Rather... at BBQLA, Los Angeles," *ArtReview*, Vol. 69, No. 4, London: ArtReview Ltd., May 2017, p. 121 [https://files.cargocollective.com/180800/Art-Review-WouldYouRather.pdf]
- Jody Zellen, "Recommendations: Kishio Suga," *Visual Art Source*, April, 2017 [https://www.visualartsource.com/index.php?page=editorial&pcID=26&aID=3938]
- Richard Speer, "The Pregnant Void," *Visual Art Source*, April, 2017 [https://www.visualartsource.com/index.php?page=editorial&pcID=17&aID=3961]
- Catherine Wagley, "5 Art Shows to See in L.A. This Week," *LA Weekly*, March 15, 2017 [https://www.laweekly.com/5-art-shows-to-see-in-l-a-this-week-3/]
- Alessandra Alliata Nobili, "Kishio Suga: Situations," *ArtAsiaPacific*, No. 102, Hong Kong: ArtAsiaPacific Publishing LLC., March–April 2017, p. 159
- 「リレーショナル・アート再考と菅木志雄、NYで美術館初個展」『美術手帖』No. 1049、美術出版社、2017年2月、pp.126–127
- 「アートはどう成立するか」『図書新聞』3286号、図書新聞、2017年1月14日、pp.1–2
- Kamini Vellodi, "Materiality Cut Two Ways," *MAP Magazine*, January, 2017 [https://mapmagazine.co.uk/materiality-cut-two-ways]
- Ionit Behar, "The world that reveals that it is a world: On The Art of Mono-ha and New Materialism," *VIS: Revista do Programa de Pós-graduação em Arte da UnB*, V. 16, nº1, Brasilia: Universidade de Brasília, janeiro-junho, 2017, pp. 66-80 [https://periodicos.unb.br/index.php/revistavis/article/view/20461/18894]
- Hanae Ko, "Five Plus One: Kishio Suga," *ArtAsiaPacific Almanac 2017*, Hong Kong: ArtAsiaPacific Publishing LLC., 2017, p. 72
- Barbara Casavecchia, "Kishio Suga: Situations," *ArtReview*, Vol. 68, No. 9, London: ArtReview Ltd., December 2016, p. 101 [https://artreview.com/december-2016-review-kishio-suga-situations/]

- Sami Emory, "Precarious Cut-Stones Sculptures Convey a Sense of Delicate Balance," *The Creators Project*, December 10, 2016 [http://thecreatorsproject2.vice.com/blog/precarious-cut-stone-sculptures]
- Nirmala Devi, "Previewed," *ArtReview Asia*, Vol. 4, No.5, London: ArtReview Ltd., Winter 2016, pp. 26–27
- Tamara Moscowitz, "Border Crossings: a New Show Pairs the Work of Hanne Darboven and Kishio Suga," *Wallpaper*, November 22, 2016 [https://www.wallpaper.com/art/hanne-darboven-and-kishio-suga-large-scale-visually-arresting-installations-open-at-dia-chelsea]
- Mike Wade, "A Show to Learn the Ropes of Making Art," *The Times*, October 21, 2016 [https://www.thetimes.co.uk/article/a-show-to-learn-the-ropes-of-making-art-9lptshzpc]
- "Kishio Suga: L'arte di costruire paesaggi destinati a svanire per sempre," *La Repubblica*, Rome: GEDI Gruppo Editoriale, October 16, 2016, pp. 50–51
- 高橋圭介「栃木・板室の旅館『大黒屋』温泉＋現代アート　感性の泉」『日本経済新聞』北関東版　2016年10月1日、41面
- Stuart Munro, "Ways to Investigate an Unknown Thing: Kishio Suga and the Enduring Nature of Mono-ha," *Mousse*, 55, Milan: Mousse Magazine and Publishing, October–November 2016, pp. 220–229 [https://www.moussemagazine.it/magazine/kishio-suga-stuart-munro-2016/]
- Ginevra Bria, "Kishio Suga debutta a Milano. Le foto della mostra all'Hangar Bicocca," *Artribune*, September 28, 2016 [https://www.artribune.com/tribnews/2016/09/kishio-suga-debutta-a-milano-le-foto-della-mostra-allhangar-bicocca/]
- Mika Yoshitake, "Kishio Suga: Situations," *Artforum*, Vol. 55, No. 1, New York: Artforum, September 2016, p. 182 [https://www.artforum.com/print/previews/201607/kishio-suga-situations-63091]
- "All'Hangar Bicocca la mostra 'Situations' di Kishio Suga," *La Repubblica*, September 2016 [https://milano.repubblica.it/tempo-libero/arte-e-fotografia/evento/all_hangar_bicocca_la_mostra_situations_di_kishio_suga-125491.html]
- "Counsel for the Month Ahead," *Even Magazine*, September 2016 [http://evenmagazine.com/even-more-september-2016/]
- "Kishio Suga's 70s throwback at Dia:Chelsea," *The Art Newspaper*, August 6, 2016 [https://www.theartnewspaper.com/2016/08/06/kishio-sugas-70s-throwback-at-diachelsea]
- 中村水絵「アーティストの皿　菅木志雄さん」『疾駆　chic』第7号、YKG publishing、2016年7月、pp.82–85
- "遥远的共鸣 菅木志雄谈罗伯特・莫里决斯," 芭莎艺术, 第13号, 北京：時尚出品, July 2016, pp.202–207
- Stuart Munro, "Reviews: Robert Morris & Kishio Suga. Blum & Poe, Los Angeles," *Art-Agenda*, May 4, 2016 [https://www.art-agenda.com/features/238675/robert-morris-kishio-suga]
- 永田晶子「モリス＆菅2人展：異色の顔合わせ　東京・原宿で来月7日まで」『毎日新聞』2016年4月6日（夕刊）、8面
- 「板室『文化味わう温泉』に　基本理念一新　芸術を前面に」『読売新聞』栃木版　2016年3月29日、31面
- Calum Sutherland, "Robert Morris and Kishio Suga," *Ocula.com*, March 17, 2016 [https://ocula.com/art-galleries/blum-poe/exhibitions/robert-morris--kishio-suga/]
- Calum Sutherland, "Robert Morris and Kishio Suga's Piece in Conversation," *Japan Times*, March 16, 2016 [https://www.japantimes.co.jp/culture/2016/03/15/arts/robert-morris-and-kishio-sugas-piece-in-conversation/]
- Taro Nettleton, "Kishio Suga," *ArtReview Asia*, Vol. 4, No. 2, London: ArtReview Ltd., March 2016, pp. 50–55
- Keisuke Mori, trans. Naoki Matsuyama, "Interview: Kishio Suga – From 'Presence' to 'Existence.'," *Bijutsutecho*, Special Issue – Spring 2016, Hong Kong: Joint Publishing (HK) Co., Ltd. / Tokyo: Gakken Holdings Co., Ltd. / Tokyo: Bijutsu Shuppan-sha Co., Ltd., pp. 52–59
- Mika Yoshitake, "Mono-ha's Afterlife," *Bijutsutecho*, Special Issue – Spring 2016, Hong Kong: Joint Publishing (HK) Co., Ltd. / Tokyo: Gakken Holdings Co., Ltd. / Tokyo: Bijutsu Shuppan-sha Co., Ltd., pp. 62–64
- Angie Kordic, "Robert Morris and Kishio Suga Installations Confronted at Blum and Poe Tokyo," *Widewalls*, February 26, 2016 [https://www.widewalls.ch/magazine/robert-morris-kishio-suga-blum-poe-tokyo]
- "Kishio Suga Wins Mainichi Art Award in Visual Arts," *Artforum.com*, January 29, 2016 [https://www.artforum.com/news/kishio-suga-wins-mainichi-art-award-in-visual-arts-57794]
- Sylvia Tsai, "Kishio Suga Wins Mainichi Art Award," *ArtAsiaPacific.com*, January 28, 2016 [http://www.artasiapacific.com/News/KishioSugaWinsMainichiArtAward]
- 「第57回毎日芸術賞決まる　現代美術家・菅木志雄氏など」『新美術新聞』No.1397、美術年鑑社、2016年1月21日、3面
- 永田晶子「毎日芸術賞の人々：3　菅木志雄さん」『毎日新聞』2016年1月6日、5面
- 「社告：第57回毎日芸術賞」『毎日新聞』2016年1月1日、1面
- 建畠晢「第57回毎日芸術賞 受賞者7人の業績　美術I部門（絵画・彫刻・グラフィック）菅木志雄さん『菅木志雄』展、『菅木志雄 置かれた潜在性』展の成果」『毎日新聞』2016年1月1日、8面
- 「2014〜2015年 私のこの3展」『aica JAPAN NEWS LETTER』（ウェブ版）第5号、美術評論家連盟、2015年12月6日発行、pp. 16–22 [https://www.aicajapan.com/newsletter_n/webnewsletter_5.pdf]
- Richard X. Zawitz, "Observation and Exploration," *World Sculpture News*, Vol. 21 No. 1, Hong Kong: Asian Art Press (International) Ltd., Winter 2015, p. 120
- 「第2特集　秋だ、旅行だ、アートに泊まろう!」『芸術新潮』第66巻第11号、新潮社、2015年11月、pp.92–109
- 「住む、の色々　菅木志雄さんを訪ねる」『疾駆　chic』第6号、YKG publishing、2015年7月、pp.46–57
- 「木や石、鉄などを手加えず表現『もの派』欧米で再注目」『河北新報』2015年6月18日、13面
- 室井俊二、小川英晴（談）「小川英晴のアート縦横 No.55　温泉文化と文化経済との高い融合をめざす、室井俊二の生き方」『ギャラリー』第362号、ギャラリーステーション、2015年6月、pp.101–109
- Andrew Maerkle, "Kishio Suga: Museum of Contemporary Art," *Frieze*, No. 172, London: Frieze Publishing Ltd., June/July/August 2015, p. 175

- Jessica Jane Howard, "Reviews: Kishio Suga: Situated Latency," *ArtAsiaPacific*, No. 93, Hong Kong: ArtAsiaPacific Publishing LLC., May–June 2015, p. 123
- *Pinault Collection*, Numéro 04, Paris: Pinault Collection, *Avril–Septembre* 2015, pp. 12–19
- 岸桂子「美術：東京、静岡の美術館で菅木志雄展　見えない世界」『毎日新聞』2015年3月11日（夕刊）、6面
- 「『もの』と等距離に対話―アーティスト・菅木志雄さん」『静岡新聞』2015年3月9日、29面
- 井上晋治「見えない領域を取り出す『もの派』菅木志雄さん個展」『読売新聞』2015年3月5日、27面
- 一井建二（聞き手）「今月のトップランナー Vol.34：菅木志雄」『アートコレクターズ』No. 72、生活の友社、2015年3月、pp. 7–10
- 倉林靖「"共震"する感覚によって、構築された世界」『いけ花龍生』第659号、一般社団法人龍生華道会、2015年3月、pp. 28–31
- 松井みどり（聞き手）「ARTIST INTERVIEW：菅木志雄　Kishio Suga」『美術手帖』No. 1019、美術出版社、2015年3月、pp. 225–239
- 赤坂英人「『もの派』が生む清々しき風景から、ものに隠れたリアリティを見る」『Pen』No. 377、CCCメディアハウス、2015年3月、p. 162
- Satoru Nagoya, "Reviews: Kishio Suga MOT, Tokyo," *Flash Art International*, Vol. 48, No. 301, Milan: Politi Editore, March–April 2015, p. 14 [https://flash---art.com/2015/04/kishio-suga-mot-tokyo/]
- 「航跡：見ることがつくること　菅木志雄さん（アーティスト）　考える主体は『もの』」『岩手日報』2015年2月28日、13面
- 黒沢綾子「2つの菅木志雄展　依存し合う『もの』の姿」『産経新聞』2015年2月26日、19面
- 岡部あおみ「美術評：菅木志雄個展　存在から輪郭引き出す」『東京新聞』2015年2月20日（夕刊）、7面
- 村田真「菅木志雄展、2会場で　再評価される『もの派』」『北海道新聞』2015年2月16日、7面
- Carter Glace, "Kishio Collection Full of Surprises, Humor," *Washington Square News*, February 10, 2015 [https://nyunews.com/2015/02/10/kishio-collection-full-of-surprises-humor/]
- 大西若人「空間生かす『もの派』場を成立させる存在 表現　菅木志雄展 東京・静岡で」『朝日新聞』2015年2月4日（夕刊）、4面
- Matin Momen, "Kishio Suga," *Style Zeitgeist*, February 4, 2015 [https://www.sz-mag.com/news/2015/02/kishio-suga]
- Jason Farago, "Kishio Suga," *New Yorker*, January 26, 2015, p. 13

作品リスト　│　List of works

凡例:
・作品のデータは、リスト番号、作品タイトル、制作
年、素材、サイズ（高さ［縦］×幅［横］×奥行）、所
蔵先、掲載ページの順に、日本語、英語で記した。
・所蔵先の記載がないものは全て作家蔵。

Notes:
・The information for each work is written in
the following order: list number, title of work,
year of production, medium, size (height ×
width × depth), collection and page number
in both Japanese and English.
・Unless otherwise noted, all works are from
the collection of the artist.

1
積層空間
Layered Space
1968
アクリル板、おがくず、綿、灰、プラスティック
屑、土
Plexiglass, sawdust, cotton, ashes,
plastic chips, soil
100.0 × 100.0 × 100.0 cm
p. 22

2
斜位相
Diagonal Phase
1969
木、石
Wood, stone
273.0 × 281.0 × 71.0 cm
p. 23

3
間状帯
Belt of Interstitial Condition
1972
木、針金、ターンバックル
Wood, wire, turnbuckle
28.0 × 115.0 × 20.0 cm
佐藤毅氏蔵
Collection of Mr. Tsuyoshi Satoh
p. 24

4
状況体
Bodies of Condition
1973
木、花崗岩、針金
Wood, granite, wire
300.0 × 1900.0 × 14.0 cm
p. 25

5
表間相
Appearance in Phase
1969 / 2012

タイプCプリント
C-print
20.0 × 28.5 cm
p. 26

6
無為状況
Inactive Environment
1970 / 2012
タイプCプリント
C-print
20.0 × 27.8 cm
p. 26

7
地因隠律
Territorial Cause, Latent Order
1972 / 2012
タイプCプリント
C-print
20.0 × 28.5 cm
p. 26

8
水上識体
Floating Units of Perception
1973 / 2012
タイプCプリント
C-print
20.0 × 28.3 cm
p. 26

9
枝況
Branched Condition
1973 / 2012
タイプCプリント
C-print
20.0 × 28.3 cm
p. 26

10
間素
Elements in Space
1973 / 2015
タイプCプリント
C-print
28.2 × 20.0 cm
p. 26

11
木状結律
Law of Wood in Connected State
1973 / 2012
タイプCプリント
C-print
20.0 × 28.4 cm
p. 26

12
識況
Condition of Perception

1970 / 2006
ゼラチン・シルバー・プリント
Gelatin silver print
89.5 × 63.5 cm
p. 27

13
界律
Space-Order
1974 / 2006
ゼラチン・シルバー・プリント
Gelatin silver print
90.0 × 60.0 cm
p. 28

14
界律
Space-Order
1974 / 2006
ゼラチン・シルバー・プリント
Gelatin silver print
90.0 × 60.0 cm
p. 29

15
等間体
In the State of Equal Dimension
1973 / 2006
ゼラチン・シルバー・プリント
Gelatin silver print
89.5 × 59.5 cm
p. 30

16
依存素
Elements of Dependency
1974 / 2015
タイプCプリント
C-print
20.0 × 28.0 cm
p. 31

17
無変律
Law of Immutability
1974 / 2015
タイプCプリント
C-print
20.0 × 28.0 cm
p. 31

18
自然律
Natural Order
1975 / 2012
タイプCプリント
C-print
20.0 × 28.0 cm
p. 31

19
留地
Fastened Earth
1975 / 2015
タイプCプリント
C-print
20.0 × 28.1 cm
p. 31

20
留位置
Fastened Placement
1975 / 2012
タイプCプリント
C-print
20.0 × 28.2 cm
p. 31

21
間留
Remaining Space
1975 / 2012
タイプCプリント
C-print
20.0 × 28.5 cm
p. 31

22
地動差
Discrepancies of Movement on the
Ground
1976 / 2012
タイプCプリント
C-print
20.0 × 27.8 cm
p. 31

23
界片
Realm of Fragments
1975
ビニール、紙、鉛筆
Vinyl, paper, pencil
36.9 × 56.6 cm
p. 32

24
依相 175
Phase of Dependence 175
1975
テープ、インク、紙
Tape, ink, paper
70.7 × 53.3 cm
小山登美夫ギャラリー蔵
Collection of Tomio Koyama Gallery
p. 33

25
線の界 212
Realm of Lines 212
1974
インク、鉛筆、紙

Ink, pencil, paper
37.6 × 54.0 cm
個人蔵
Private collection
p. 34

26
線の界 211
Realm of Lines 211
1975
インク、紙
Ink, paper
37.6 × 54.0 cm
個人蔵
Private collection
p. 34

27
線の界 216
Realm of Lines 216
1975
クレパス、紙
Oil pastel, paper
37.6 × 53.9 cm
個人蔵
Private collection
p. 34

28
線の界 217
Realm of Lines 217
1975
クレパス、テープ、紙
Oil pastel, tape, paper
37.6 × 54.0 cm
個人蔵
Private collection
p. 34

29
線の界 217
Realm of Lines 217
1975
クレパス、テープ、ビニールテープ、紙
Oil pastel, tape, vinyl tape, paper
37.6 × 54.0 cm
個人蔵
Private collection
p. 34

30
線の界 207
Realm of Lines 207
1975
クレパス、クラフトテープ、紙
Oil pastel, craft tape, paper
39.6 × 54.5 cm
個人蔵
Private collection
p. 34

31
線の界 204
Realm of Lines 204
1976
クレパス、紙
Oil pastel, paper
37.7 × 54.0 cm
個人蔵
Private collection
p. 35

32
線の界 205
Realm of Lines 205
1976
鉛筆、クレパス、ビニールテープ、紙
Pencil, oil pastel, vinyl tape, paper
39.5 × 54.6 cm
個人蔵
Private collection
p. 35

33
線の界 203
Realm of Lines 203
1976
クレパス、テープ、紙
Oil pastel, tape, paper
54.0 × 37.6 cm
個人蔵
Private collection
p. 35

34
離空
Divergent Space
1975
木、セメントブロック
Wood, cement block
184.0 × 216.0 × 456.0 cm
p. 36

35
領空
Territorial Void
1978
段ボール紙、パステル
Cardboard, pastel
23.6 × 51.0 cm
p. 38

36
過中
Passing the Interior
1978
段ボール紙
Cardboard
31.3 × 32.9 cm
p. 38

37
域場
Area of Site
1979
ハトロン紙、鉛筆、紙
Kraft paper, pencil, paper
37.7 × 59.8 cm
p. 39

38
界囲構
Enclosed Space
1980
紙、鉛筆
Paper, pencil
50.5 × 48.5 cm
p. 40

39
集為論
Theory of Gathering
1980
紙、鉛筆
Paper, pencil
52.5 × 49.5 cm
p. 40

40
対空
Confronting Spaces
1980
鉛筆、紙
Paper, pencil
56.1 × 64.4 cm
p. 40

41
在置向
Existence of Placed Orientation
1981
封筒、アクリルペイント、鉛筆
Envelope, acrylic paint, pencil
61.5 × 43.0 cm
p. 41

42
作用空
Effects of Voids
1982
封筒、アクリルペイント
Envelope, acrylic paint
58.0 × 43.0 cm
p. 41

43
切り取られた分間
Separation of Divided Intervals
1982
封筒、アクリルペイント、鉛筆
Envelope, acrylic paint, pencil
61.6 × 43.0 cm
p. 41

44
占められた領辺
Occupied Territory and Edges
1982
封筒、アクリルペイント
Envelope, acrylic paint
61.6 × 43.0 cm
p. 41

45
事位
Matter and Location
1980
木、枝、紙、亜鉛メッキ鋼板、石
Wood, branch, paper, galvanized iron
plate, stones
245.0 × 583.0 × 540.0 cm
pp.42–43

46
AS FACTS–1
1980
紙、パステル
Paper, pastel
59.0 × 89.0 cm
p. 44

47
AS FACTS–10
1980
紙、パステル
Paper, pastel
53.1 × 58.6 cm
p. 44

48
臨界面 081
Surface of Critical Boundary 081
1981
サンドペーパー、チョーク
Sand paper, chalk
44.5 × 54.5 cm
佐藤毅氏蔵
Collection of Mr. Tsuyoshi Satoh
p. 45

49
D系列
The Series D
1982
木
Wood
55.5 × 223.5 × 4.5 cm
小山登美夫ギャラリー蔵
Collection of Tomio Koyama Gallery
p. 46

50
集の支え
Support of Accumulation
1983
木

Wood
153.0 × 152.8 × 34.4 cm
p. 47

51
内側の作用　No. 4
Effects of Interior No. 4
1985
亜鉛メッキ鋼板、ペイント、木
Galvanized iron plate, paint, wood
11.0 × 11.1 × 4.3 cm
個人蔵
Private collection
p. 48

52
内側の作用　No. 3
Effects of Interior No. 3
1985
亜鉛メッキ鋼板、紙
Galvanized iron plate, paper
65.0 × 71.5 × 40.5 cm
個人蔵
Private collection
p. 48

53
スクエアポンド
Square Pond
1986
亜鉛メッキ鋼板
Colored galvanized iron plate
79.0 × 107.0 × 7.0 cm
小山登美夫ギャラリー蔵
Collection of Tomio Koyama Gallery
p. 49

54
縁辺消失
Disappearance of Edges and Sides
1986–1987
木、ペイント
Wood, paint
67.0 × 49.0 × 8.2 cm
岩手県立美術館蔵
Collection of Iwate Museum of Art
p. 50

55
PROTRUSION ZX87
1987
木、オイルペイント
Wood, oil paint
63.0 × 95.0 × 9.0 cm
個人蔵
Private collection
p. 52

56
PROTRUSION 000
1987
木、ラッカー

Wood, lacquer
106.0 × 19.0 × 19.0 cm
個人蔵
Private collection
p. 53

57
PROTRUSION HX87
1987
木、ラッカー
Wood, lacquer
106.0 × 19.0 × 19.0 cm
個人蔵
Private collection
p. 53

58
無端
No Edge
1983
水彩、鉛筆、紙
Water color, pencil, paper
76.5 × 55.0 cm
p. 54

59
無在
No Existence
1983
水彩、鉛筆、紙
Water color, pencil, paper
76.5 × 55.0 cm
p. 54

60
無題
Untitled
1985
水彩、鉛筆、紙
Water color, pencil, paper
79.0 × 109.5 cm
p. 55

61
無題
Untitled
1985
水彩、鉛筆、紙
Water color, pencil, paper
79.0 × 109.5 cm
p. 55

62
無題
Untitled
1985
水彩、鉛筆、紙
Water color, pencil, paper
79.5 × 109.0 cm
p. 55

63
補われた素材−58
Supplemented Material−58
1984
木、パテ
Wood, putty
90.0 × 90.5 × 3.0 cm
個人蔵
Private collection
p. 56

64
景集素
Scene of Gathered Elements
1984−1991
木、アクリルペイント
Wood, acrylic paint
45.0 × 43.6 × 7.3 cm
p. 57

65
周切囲合
Surrounded Separation and Enclosed
Conjunction
1988
木、鉄
Wood, iron
69.4 × 50.1 × 9.5 cm
p. 57

66
上弦・間・下弦
Waxing-Space-Waning
1990
木、石、紐
Wood, stone, rope
210.0 × 500.0 × 60.0 cm
pp. 58–59

67
離図周界
Separated Diagram, Surrounding Realm
1990
木、アクリルペイント
Wood, acrylic paint
162.5 × 117.0 × 11.0 cm
p. 60

68
距離の定位
Determined Position of Distance
1990
木、鉄、アクリルペイント
Wood, iron, acrylic paint
41.5 × 17.4 × 31.0 cm
p. 62

69
永遠のコーナー
Corner of Eternity
1990
木、アルミ、アクリルペイント

Wood, aluminum, acrylic paint
31.1 × 31.3 × 9.4 cm
p. 62

70
木の側界
Lateral Realm of Wood
1990
木、アクリルペイント
Wood, acrylic paint
30.3 × 72.8 × 3.8 cm
p. 63

71
縁を支える二つの木
Two Trees Supporting the Edges
1990
木、アクリルペイント
Wood, acrylic paint
201.8 × 121.8 × 14.5 cm
佐藤毅氏蔵
Collection of Mr. Tsuyoshi Satoh
p. 64

72
囲間内奥
Surrounded Spaces of Interior Depth
1991
亜鉛メッキ鋼板、木
Galvanized iron plate, wood
65.0 × 63.0 × 7.7 cm
岩手県立美術館蔵
Collection of Iwate Museum of Art
p. 65

73
叙々に
By Degrees
1990
封筒、アクリルペイント、鉛筆
Envelope, acrylic paint, pencil
33.5 × 21.0 cm
p. 66

74
そこまではいく
Go as Far as There
1990
封筒、アクリルペイント、ガムテープ
Envelope, acrylic paint, duct tape
30.5 × 23.5 cm
p. 66

75
water band
1990
紙袋、アクリルペイント、鉛筆、亜鉛メッキ鋼
板
Paper bag, acrylic paint, pencil,
galvanized iron plate
38.5 × 31.5 cm
p. 66

76
紙構露景
Composition of Paper, Revealed Scenery
1990
段ボール紙、アクリルペイント、テープ
Cardboard, acrylic paint, tape
38.5 × 38.0 cm
p. 66

77
集場（5）
Accumulation of Sites (5)
1992
新聞紙、インク
Newspaper, ink
54.4 × 39.0 cm
p. 67

78
集場（7）
Accumulation of Sites (7)
1992
新聞紙、インク
Newspaper, ink
52.4 × 39.3 cm
p. 67

79
集場（6）
Accumulation of Sites (6)
1992
新聞紙、インク
Newspaper, ink
54.0 × 32.0 cm
p. 67

80
無空
Without Void
1993
インク、紙
Ink, paper
54.7 × 40.0 cm
p. 68

81
無空空
Void Without Void
1993
インク、紙
Ink, paper
54.7 × 40.0 cm
p. 68

82
体の素因
Factors of Body
1993
木、アクリルペイント、針金、ネジ
Wood, acrylic paint, wire, screw
74.5 × 39.0 × 5.5 cm
p. 69

83
端の識景
Perceived Scenery of Extremities
1993
木、アクリルペイント、針金、ネジ
Wood, acrylic paint, wire, screw
64.0 × 44.0 × 5.0 cm
p. 69

84
無化景結
Nullification of Scenic Connections
1995
木、アクリルペイント
Wood, acrylic paint
202.5 × 257.5 × 8.0 cm
p. 70

85
縦横構縁
Composition of Length and Width
1996
亜鉛メッキ鋼板波板
Galvanized corrugated sheet
63.0 × 62.0 × 11.0 cm
p. 71

86
周集系
System of Surroundings
1998
木、スチールパイプ、スチール棒
Wood, steel pipes, steel rods
212.0 × 410.0 × 600.0 cm
pp. 72–73

87
大地の育成
The Cultivation of Mother Earth
2000
パイプ、バケツ、木箱、砕石、ロープ
Steel pipes, buckets, wooden box,
crushed stones, rope
228.0×310.0×935.0 cm
pp. 74–75

88
内境然因
Interior Boundaries and Natural Causes
2001
鉄
Iron
54.0 × 43.0 × 5.7 cm
岩手県立美術館蔵
Collection of Iwate Museum of Art
p. 76

89
端片移差
Edges of Fragments and Transitional
Discrepancies
2001

ガラス、木、接着剤、ペイント
Glass, wood, glue, acrylic paint
55.0 × 60.0 × 2.4 cm
岩手県立美術館蔵
Collection of Iwate Museum of Art
p. 77

90
共地
Concurrent Ground
2008
木、アクリルペイント
Wood, acrylic paint
182.0 × 91.0 × 4.5 cm
p. 78

91
組みかえられた斜向
Recombined Diagonal Orientation
2005
木、アクリルペイント
Wood, acrylic paint
37.5 × 54.5 × 3.0 cm
個人蔵
Private collection
p. 79

92
臨中集散
Critical Interior and Gathered
Dispersion
2003
木、アクリルペイント
Wood, acrylic paint
110.0 × 108.0 × 10.0 cm
p. 79

93
揺間
Oscillating Spaces
2005
ビニールシート、レーザー、木、ペイント、ワイヤー
Vinyl sheets, laser, wood, paint, wire
580.0 × 766.5 × 2003.0 cm
岩手県立美術館蔵
Collection of Iwate Museum of Art
p. 80

94
集向
Gathered Orientations
2005
釣竿、石、コンクリートブロック、紐、砂利、
ラッカー
Fishing rods, stones, concrete blocks,
string, gravel, lacquer
522.0 × 766.0 × 2200.0 cm
岩手県立美術館蔵
Collection of Iwate Museum of Art
p. 81

95
散立
Dispersed Emergence
2005
パイプ、アルミ足場板、木、砂利
Steel pipes, aluminium scaffold planks,
wood, gravel
262.8 × 1830.0 × 3100.0 cm
岩手県立美術館蔵
Collection of Iwate Museum of Art
p. 82

96
対応
Correspondence
2006
木、石、ビニール紐
Wood, stone, vinyl rope
318.0 × 400.0 × 31.0 cm
p. 83

97
複潜化−5
Multiple Latencies in Formation−5
2007
木、アクリルペイント
Wood, acrylic paint
243.0 × 122.0 × 6.8 cm
p. 84

98
複潜在
Multiple Latencies in Existence
2007
木、アクリルペイント
Wood, acrylic paint
243.0 × 122.0 × 6.8 cm
p. 84

99
複潜化−6
Multiple Latencies in Formation−6
2007
木、アクリルペイント
Wood, acrylic paint
243.0 × 122.0 × 6.8 cm
p. 85

100
間を縮める
Shortening the Interstices
2006
木、石、鉄、紐
Wood, stones, iron, rope
140.0 × 300.0 × 110.0 cm
p. 86

101
間状化.
Spacing Situation
2010
木、アクリルペイント、セメント

Wood, acrylic paint, cement
163.0 × 71.0 × 38.0 cm
p. 87

102
連集個
Connecting Surroundings and Individuals
2010−2011
木、アクリルペイント
Wood, acrylic paint
200.0 × 200.0 × 13.0 cm
個人蔵
Private collection
p. 88

103
無間静限
Nullification of Intervals and Reposed Limit
2011
アクリルペイント、木、画布
Acrylic paint, wood, canvas
194.0 × 162.5 × 4.5 cm
p. 89

104
空止耕
Halted and Cultivated Space
2017
木、石
Wood, stones
68.0 × 652.0 × 254.0 cm
pp. 90−91

105
止域
Halted Areas
2016
木、アクリルペイント
Wood, acrylic paint
142.0 × 118.5 × 11.0 cm
p. 92

106
連場
Connected Sites
2017
木、アクリルペイント
Wood, acrylic paint
187.0 × 150.5 × 9.0 cm
p. 92

107
潜因空
Space of Latent Cause
2017
木、アクリルペイント
Wood, acrylic paint
182.0 × 136.5 × 10.0 cm
p. 93

108
所成性
Location of Composition
2017
木、アクリルペイント
Wood, acrylic paint
190.5 × 158.5 × 14.0 cm
p. 94

109
超間
Beyond Space
2018
木、アクリルペイント
Wood, acrylic paint
187.3 × 141.0 × 19.0 cm
p. 95

110
縁立
Arising Edges
2018
木、アクリルペイント
Wood, acrylic paint
217.0 × 144.5 × 12.4 cm
p. 96

111
揺化律
Law of Oscillation
2018
木、アクリルペイント
Wood, acrylic paint
182.0 × 133.5 × 13.3 cm
p. 97

112
深差
Depth of Discrepancies
2019
木、アクリルペイント
Wood, acrylic paint
180.0 × 134.9 × 13.7 cm
p. 98

113
景素
Scene of Elements
2020
木、アクリルペイント
Wood, acrylic paint
181.0 × 135.0 × 9.4 cm
p. 99

114
潜深
Latent Depths
2018
木、アクリルペイント、石
Wood, acrylic paint, stone
255.1 × 95.7 × 82.3 cm
p.100

謝辞

Acknowledgements

本展の開催および本書の刊行にあたり、多大なご協力を賜りました下記の諸機関、関係者の皆様に深甚なる感謝の意を表します。また、ここにお名前を記すことはできませんでしたが、本展実現のため格別のご尽力を賜りました方々に心から感謝申し上げます。
（敬称略・順不同）

We would like to express our sincere gratitude to all the following for their generous assistance and contributions to the realization of this exhibition and book. We are also very grateful to those who kindly supported us but wish to remain anonymous, and to all who have assisted in the preparation of the exhibition.

菅木志雄

Kishio Suga

小山登美夫ギャラリー

Tomio Koyama Gallery

ギャラリー彩園子
慶応義塾大学アート・センター
株式会社ツァイト・フォト
東京画廊+BTAP
横浜市民ギャラリー
Blum & Poe
IBC岩手放送

Blum & Poe
Gallery Saiensu
Iwate Broadcasting, Co., Ltd.
Keio University Art Center
Tokyo Gallery + BTAP
Yokohama Civic Art Gallery
Zeit-Foto Co., Ltd.

天野太郎
安齊セツ子
大塚真弓
小笠原卓雄
加藤弘子
金子多朔
金子太郎
久保仁志
佐藤毅
杉本吉武
鈴木郷史
鈴木利佳
関直子
建畠晢
手塚一郎
中村麗子
橋本尚恣
長谷川誠
細野泰久
松永真太郎
宮澤明裕
村井睦平
室井俊二
森啓輔
山根佳奈

Taro Amano
Setsuko Anzai
Makoto Hasegawa
Naotsugu Hashimoto
Yasuhisa Hosono
Taro Kaneko
Tasaku Kaneko
Hiroko Kato
Hitoshi Kubo
Shintaro Matsunaga
Akihiro Miyazawa
Keisuke Mori
Rikuhei Murai
Shunji Muroi
Reiko Nakamura
Takuo Ogasawara
Mayumi Otsuka
Tsuyoshi Satoh
Naoko Seki
Yoshitake Sugimoto
Rika Suzuki
Satoshi Suzuki
Akira Tatehata
Ichiro Tezuka
Kana Yamane

本書は下記の展覧会に関連して出版されました。

開館20周年記念
菅木志雄展 〈もの〉の存在と〈場〉の永遠

会期：2021年12月18日（土）-2022年2月20日（日）
会場：岩手県立美術館
主催：岩手県立美術館、公益財団法人岩手県文化振興事業団
後援：一般社団法人岩手県芸術文化協会、
岩手県商工会議所連合会、岩手日報社、岩手日日新聞社、
盛岡タイムス社、NHK盛岡放送局、IBC岩手放送、テレビ岩手、
めんこいテレビ、岩手朝日テレビ、エフエム岩手、
ラヂオ・もりおか、岩手ケーブルテレビジョン、情報紙ゆうゆう
協力：ギャラリー彩園子、東京画廊＋BTAP、Blum & Poe
企画協力：小山登美夫ギャラリー
作品輸送：大宝運輸
作品展示：日本通運、株式会社サンフィード
グラフィック・デザイン：林琢真（林琢真デザイン事務所）
広報印刷物製作：永代印刷株式会社
看板製作：株式会社サンフィード

This book is published as the catalogue of the following exhibition.

20th Anniversary of the Iwate Museum of Art
Kishio Suga: The Existence of "Things" and the Eternity of "Site"

Period: December 18, 2021 – February 20, 2022
Venue: Iwate Museum of Art
Organized by: Iwate Museum of Art, Iwate Cultural Promotion Agency
Supported by: Iwate Prefectural Artistic And Cultural Association, Federation of Chambers of Commerce and Industry in Iwate Prefecture, Iwate Nippo Co., Ltd., Iwate Nichinichi Shimbun, Morioka Times, Iwate Broadcasting, Co., Ltd., Television Iwate Corp., Iwate Menkoi Television Co., Ltd., Iwate Asahi TV Co., Ltd., FM Iwate Broadcasting Company, Radio Morioka Corporation, Iwate Cable Television, Free paper yuuyuu
In cooperation with: Gallery Saiensu, Tokyo Gallery + BTAP, Blum & Poe
In curatorial cooperation with: Tomio Koyama Gallery
Transportation: Taiho Unyu Co. Ltd.
Installation: Nippon Express, 3Feed Co., Ltd.
Graphic design: Takuma Hayashi (Hayashi Takuma Design Office)
Public relations publications printed by: Eidai Printing Co., Ltd.
Signboard installation: 3Feed Co., Ltd.

撮影：

いわねスタジオ　pp. 34-35, 48, 79上
内田芳孝　pp. 83, 86
岡野圭　p. 53
木奥恵三　pp. 49, 55
坂本理　pp. 32, 57上, 62-63
佐藤毅　pp. 58-59, 74-75
菅木志雄　pp. 22, 25
髙橋健治　pp. 23-24, 33, 36, 38, 45-47, 56-57, 60, 64, 66, 69-73, 78, 90-100
橋本尚恣　pp. 3, 42-43
武藤滋生　p. 52
渡辺郁弘　pp. 39-41, 44, 54, 67-68, 79下, 84-85, 87-89

Photographer:

Naotsugu Hashimoto pp. 3, 42-43
Iwane Studio pp. 34-35, 48, 79 above
Keizo Kioku pp. 49, 55
Shigeo Muto p. 52
Kei Okano p. 53
Osamu Sakamoto pp. 32, 57 above, 62-63
Tsuyoshi Satoh pp. 58-59, 74-75
Kishio Suga pp. 22, 25
Kenji Takahashi pp. 23-24, 33, 36, 38, 45-47, 56-57, 60, 64, 66, 69-73, 78, 90-100
Yoshitaka Uchida pp. 83, 86
Ikuhiro Watanabe pp. 39-41, 44, 54, 67-68, 79 below, 84-85, 87-89

写真提供・協力：

岩手県立美術館　pp. 34-35, 48, 50, 65, 76-77, 79上, 80-82
ギャラリー彩園子　pp. 3, 42-43
小山登美夫ギャラリー　pp. 22-24, 26-33, 36, 38-41, 44-47, 49, 54-60, 62-64, 66-73, 78, 79下, 83-100
佐藤毅　p. 25
東京画廊＋BTAP　pp. 53, 74-75

Courtesy:

Gallery Saiensu pp. 3, 42-43
Iwate Museum of Art pp. 34-35, 48, 50, 65, 76-77, 79 above, 80-82
Tsuyoshi Satoh p. 25
Tokyo Gallery + BTAP pp. 53, 74-75
Tomio Koyama Gallery pp. 22-24, 26-33, 36, 38-41, 44-47, 49, 54-60, 62-64, 66-73, 78, 79 below, 83-100

菅木志雄 〈もの〉の存在と〈場〉の永遠

発行日：2021年12月18日　第1刷

執筆：菅木志雄、建畠晢（多摩美術大学学長）、濱淵真弓（岩手県立美術館上席専門学芸員）
翻訳：ダリル・ウィー（pp. 5, 15–19, 104–107, 111–113）、藤川二葉（p. 9）
英文校閲：アシュレイ・ローリングス（Blum & Poe）

デザイン：林琢真（林琢真デザイン事務所）
編集：岩手県立美術館、小山登美夫ギャラリー、HeHe
編集協力：佐藤毅

協力：ギャラリー彩園子、東京画廊＋BTAP、Blum & Poe

発行者：中村水絵
発行所：HeHe／ヒヒ
〒150-0022 東京都渋谷区恵比寿南3-3-11 パラシオン恵比寿1101
Tel & Fax：03-6303-4042　info@hehepress.com　www.hehepress.com

印刷・製本所：株式会社山田写真製版所

乱丁・落丁本は送料小社負担にてお取り替えいたします。
本書の無断複写・複製・引用及び構成順序を損ねる無断使用を禁じます。

Printed in Japan

Kishio Suga: The Existence of "Things" and the Eternity of "Site"

Texts by Kishio Suga, Akira Tatehata (President, Tama Art University) and Mayumi Hamabuchi (Curator, Iwate Museum of Art)
Translated by Darryl Jingwen Wee (pp. 5–19, 104–107, 111–113) and Futaba Fujikawa (p. 9)
English proofreading by Ashley Rawlings (Blum & Poe)

Design by Takuma Hayashi (Hayashi Takuma Design Office)
Edited by Iwate Museum of Art, Tomio Koyama Gallery and HeHe
Editorial support by Tsuyoshi Satoh

In cooperation with Gallery Saiensu, Tokyo Gallery+BTAP and Blum & Poe

First published in Japan, December 2021

Published by Mizue Nakamura
HeHe
3-3-11 #1101 Ebisu-minami, Shibuya-ku, Tokyo 150-0022 Japan
Tel & Fax: +81(0)3-6303-4042　info@hehepress.com　www.hehepress.com

All rights reserved.

Printed and bound in Japan by Yamada Photo Process Co., Ltd.